AIRPLANES

The Lure of Flight

These and other books are included in the
Encyclopedia of Discovery and Invention
series:

AIRPLANES

The Lure of Flight

by TOM STACEY

The ENCYCLOPEDIA of
D·I·S·C·O·V·E·R·Y
and INVENTION

P.O. Box 289011 SAN DIEGO, CA 92128-9011

Library of Congress Cataloging-in-Publication Data

Stacey, Thomas, 1960–
    Airplanes: the lure of flight/by Tom Stacey.
      p. cm.— (The Encyclopedia of discovery and invention)
    Includes bibliographical references and index.
    Summary: Surveys the history, development, and future of
airplanes, and examines the impact of flight on civilization.
    ISBN 1-56006-203-7
    1. Aeronautics—Juvenile literature. 2. Airplanes—Juvenile
literature. [1. Aeronautics. 2. Airplanes.] I. Title
II. Series
TL547.S73 1990   90-6471
629.13—dc20   CIP
                                                  AC

Contents

. . . .

Foreword

The belief in progress has been one of the dominant forces in Western Civilization from the Scientific Revolution of the seventeenth century to the present. Embodied in the idea of progress is the conviction that each generation will be better off than the one that preceded it. Eventually, all peoples will benefit from and share in this better world. R. R. Palmer, in his *History of the Modern World*, calls this belief in progress "a kind of nonreligious faith that the conditions of human life" will continually improve as time goes on.

For over a thousand years prior to the seventeenth century, science had progressed little. Inquiry was largely discouraged, and experimentation almost nonexistent. As a result, science became regressive and discovery was ignored. Benjamin Farrington, a historian of science, characterized it this way: "Science had failed to become a real force in the life of society. Instead there had arisen a conception of science as a cycle of liberal studies for a privileged minority. Science ceased to be a means of transforming the conditions of life." In short, had this intellectual climate continued, humanity's future world would have been little more than a clone of its past.

Fortunately, these circumstances were not destined to last. By the seventeenth and eighteenth centuries, Western society was undergoing radical and favorable changes. And the changes that occurred gave rise to the notion that progress was a real force urging civilization forward. Surpluses of consumer goods were replacing substandard living conditions in most of Western Europe. Rigid class systems were giving way to social mobility. In nations like France and the United States, the lofty principles of democracy and popular sovereignty were being painted in broad, gilded strokes over the fading canvasses of monarchy and despotism.

But more significant than these social, economic, and political changes, the new age witnessed a rebirth of science. Centuries of scientific stagnation began crumbling before a spirit of scientific inquiry that spawned undreamed of technological advances. And it was the discoveries and inventions of scores of men and women that fueled these new technologies, dramatically increasing the ability of humankind to control nature—and, many believed, eventually to guide it.

It is a truism of science and technology that the results derived from observation and experimentation are not finalities. They are part of a process. Each discovery is but one piece in a continuum bridging past and present and heralding an extraordinary future. The heroic age of the Scientific Revolution was simply a start. It laid a foundation upon which succeeding generations of imaginative thinkers could build. It kindled the belief that progress is possible as long as there were gifted men and women who would respond to society's needs. When Antonie van Leeuwenhoek observed *Animalcules* (little animals) through his high-powered microscope in 1683, the discovery did not end there. Others followed who would call these "little animals" bacteria and, in time, recognize their role in the process of health and disease. Robert Koch, a German bacteriologist and winner of the Nobel prize in Physiology and Medicine, was one of these men. Koch firmly established that bacteria are responsible for causing infectious diseases. He identified, among others, the causative organisms of anthrax and tuberculosis. Alexander Fleming, another Nobel Laureate, progressed still further in the quest to understand and control bacteria. In 1928, Fleming discovered penicillin, the antibiotic wonder drug. Penicillin, and the generations of antibiotics that succeeded it, have done more to prevent premature death than any other discovery in the history of humankind. And as civilization hastens toward the twenty-first century, most agree that the conquest of van Leeuwenhoek's "little animals" will continue.

The *Encyclopedia of Discovery and Invention* examines those discoveries and inventions that have had a sweeping impact on life and thought in the modern world. Each book explores the ideas that led to the invention or discovery, and, more importantly, how the world changed and continues to change because of it. The series also highlights the people behind the achievements—the unique men and women whose singular genius and rich imagination have altered the lives of everyone. Enhanced by photographs and clearly explained technical drawings, these books are comprehensive examinations of the building blocks of human progress.

AIRPLANES

The Lure of Flight

AIRPLANES

Introduction

The first controlled, powered flight by humankind took place at Kitty Hawk, North Carolina, on December 17, 1903. That day Wilbur and Orville Wright did something that almost no one thought could be done. They each flew briefly, then returned safely to earth, using a motorized flying machine they designed and built themselves.

Many others had tried to fly long before the Wright brothers. Some were able to float and glide but never to fly. Most people throughout history felt certain that human flight was impossible and that it was foolish even to try. Flying in the face of doubt and skepticism, however, the Wrights achieved a techni-

... TIMELINE: AIRPLANES

1 ■ 1500
Leonardo da Vinci sketches plans for ornithopter.

2 ■ 1664
Sir Isaac Newton discovers the law of gravity.

3 ■ 1783
Joseph and Etienne Montgolfier of France invent the hot air balloon and make several flights around Paris.

4 ■ 1843
William Henson receives a patent for his aerial steam carriage.

5 ■ 1854
Sir George Cayley, the "father of aerodynamics," persuades his carriage driver to operate one of his gliders. The flight is successful.

6 ■ 1871
Frenchman Alphonse Penaud designs and builds a stable, twenty-inch glider powered by a rubber band.

7 ■ 1896
After more than two thousand flights, Otto Lilienthal dies as the result of injuries sustained in a glider crash. In Dayton, Ohio, Wilbur and Orville Wright take note and begin thinking about the problem of flight.

8 ■ August 1903
a. Professor Samuel B. Langley's aerodrome is launched over the Potomac River, with Charles Manly as pilot. The aerodrome immediately goes nose-down into the river.

b. December 17, 1903
The Wrights make several controlled, powered flights with the *Wright Flyer I* on the beach at Kitty Hawk.

9 ■ 1908
Alexander Graham Bell and Glenn Curtiss team up to produce the *June Bug*.

10 ■ 1911
Former college football star Cal Rodgers pilots the *Vin Fiz* from coast to coast in an advertising promotion for the Armour Meat Packing Company.

11 ■ 1914
World War I begins in Europe. Airplanes are first used to scout enemy troop movements.

12 ■ 1915
The first fighter plane, the French-made Moraine-Saulnier Bullet, appears.

13 ■ 1918
Airmail service begins between Washington, D.C., and New York City.

14 ■ 1924
The Douglas World Cruisers *New Orleans* and *Chicago* go around the world in 174 days.

cal triumph that still affects us today.

The airplane has become an essential part of our society. Its invention extended the reach of travelers and allowed cargo to be sent all over the world quickly. The airplane has also been an inspiration, to those who love the freedom of flying and to anyone who has tried to achieve something that others consider impossible.

The original airplane has been improved upon, of course. As it has evolved, so have the possibilities for humankind. No longer limited to the earth, we now reach for new challenges beyond our planet. The Wrights' invention opened the door to outer space exploration. It has allowed people to escape the constraints of earth and chase new dreams across the sky.

12 13 14 15 16 17 18 19 20 21 22 23 24 25 26 27

15 ■ 1927
Charles Lindbergh flies the *Spirit of St. Louis* solo from New York to Paris in 33 1/2 hours.

16 ■ 1932
Amelia Earhart flies from Newfoundland to Ireland. Later in the year she flies solo across the United States.

17 ■ 1933
The Douglas DC-3 passenger airliner is introduced in the United States.

18 ■ 1939
Germany deploys a secret air force, the *Luftwaffe*, to attack Poland. Britain and France react against Germany, and World War II is started.

19 ■ 1941
British scientists, working with Frank Whittle's Power Jets Limited, develop the Gloster E 28/39 experimental jet aircraft.

20 ■ June 6, 1944
The Allied forces invade Europe, relying heavily upon the B-17 Flying Fortress.

21 ■ August 14, 1945
The B-29 Superfortress *Enola Gay* brings an end to the war by dropping an atomic bomb on Hiroshima, Japan.

22 ■ September 17, 1947
a. President Harry S. Truman signs legislation to create the U.S. Air Force.

b. October 14, 1947
Chuck Yeager breaks the sound barrier, flying at a speed of 670 miles per hour over the California desert in the rocket-powered X-1.

23 ■ 1954
In the United States, the Boeing 707, the first large passenger jet, is introduced.

24 ■ October 4, 1957
The Soviet Union launches the first earth-orbiting satellite, *Sputnik 1*.

25 ■ July 21, 1969
U.S. astronaut Neil Armstrong becomes the first person to set foot on the moon.

26 ■ 1971
The controversial SST project is canceled in the United States. Development continues on the joint British-French SST and the Russian SST.

27 ■ January 28, 1986
a. The *Challenger* explodes seventy-three seconds into its mission, killing all seven crew members aboard.

b. December, 1986
Dick Rutan and Jeanna Yeager fly nonstop around the world without refueling in *Voyager*, designed by Burt Rutan.

The Dream of Flight

People dreamed of flying centuries before human flight was possible. They looked to the sky for freedom and excitement and imagined gliding toward the horizon like birds. The world would be a much different place if people could soar high above fields and trees, over mountains and lakes, suspended above the earth. Like eagles, they would be able to see for miles around. They would have the freedom to take off anytime, and flying would be much faster than walking. Flying would add fun and thrills to their pedestrian lives. But for most of human history, flying was only a dream.

Ancient Greek mythology tells of humanity's desire to fly. Daedalus, a mythological character, was a craftsman and inventor who experimented with flight. According to legend, he used wax, feathers, and thread to make wings for himself and his son, Icarus. They attached the wings to their bodies and flew away high into the sky. But Icarus flew too close to the sun. When his wings melted, he fell to his death in the sea. Daedalus landed in Sicily, where he never forgot the lesson: only the gods could fly.

In another case, the idea of falling from great heights motivated people to experiment with flight. Chinese officials used flight to punish criminals and deter crime. In the 1200s, the explorer Marco Polo reported that the Chinese used large kites to lift outlaws high up into the air as a form of punishment. The fear of falling from so far up presumably stopped other people from committing crimes.

Da Vinci's Early Design

Legends and myths about people wanting to fly have appeared in virtually every culture throughout world history. In some cases, people strapped on wings, as Daedalus did, and tried to fly by imitating birds. This method did not work. Birds and insects could flit

An illustration depicts the Greek myth of Daedalus and Icarus who fly towards the sun using hand-crafted wings.

from place to place, but human beings seemed to belong on the ground.

In the late 1600s, Sir Isaac Newton explained what everyone who had tried to fly knew only too well: on earth, what goes up must come down—immediately. Gravity, the attraction of a smaller object to a larger object, was one of the forces that governed humankind and the universe.

About one hundred years before Newton discovered this law of gravity, Leonardo da Vinci had turned his brilliant mind to the idea of human flight. Like others before him, the Italian painter, sculptor, musician, and scientist looked to birds for a clue. Instead of simply imitating them, however, da Vinci studied the movements of birds and analyzed how they were able to fly. He then dissected some birds and discovered that they have light, hollow bones and sinewy, powerful muscles. Human beings did not have the same kind of body structure and were clearly not equipped to fly.

Da Vinci was not discouraged, however. If humans could not achieve flight with their bodies, perhaps they could do so with a machine. Maybe he could construct a flying machine, thought da Vinci. Why not? He made sketches of such a flying machine, applying what he had learned while studying birds. He called the machine an "ornithopter." It would have space for one person to lie down, and its wings would flap like a bird's. Although da Vinci never actually built his flying machine, his ideas were on the right track. His remarkably detailed drawings revealed features similar to the airplane the Wright brothers built four hundred years later.

Dozens of other people pursued the elusive dream of human flight during

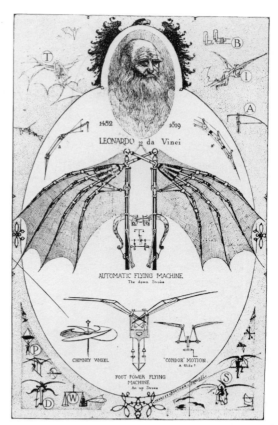

This detailed sketch by Leonardo da Vinci depicts his preoccupation with human flight and the laws of nature.

the centuries between da Vinci's brainstorm and the Wright brothers' first flight. Some of these experimenters made serious attempts to fly. Several added important contributions to the growing body of knowledge about the development and design of airplanes. This body of knowledge became known as aviation.

The Montgolfiers' Balloon

After the unwilling Chinese prisoners, the next people to achieve recorded human flight were the Montgolfier brothers, Joseph and Etienne, of France. They invented the hot air balloon in 1783. As legend has it, Joseph was sitting idly at home one day when he noticed that the smoke from the fireplace was rising to the ceiling. He borrowed some silk from the housekeeper and made a small bag with an open bottom. He then held it over the fire and watched as it went straight up.

Applying the same principle outside the house, the Montgolfier brothers built a large fire, then placed a linen bag lined with paper above the fire. Like the small bag over the fireplace, the large linen bag lifted into the sky. It was an important discovery, and the brothers did not stop there. They continued their experiments, using lightweight straw to build roaring fires in a container attached to the balloon. They sent up several of their large bags. Soon, people all over France were talking about the brothers' wonderful flying balloons.

Before long, the rulers of France, Louis XVI and Marie Antoinette, wanted to see this amazing new invention. The Montgolfiers obliged and arranged

The Montgolfier brothers launch the first hot-air balloon in France in 1783.

to perform a special balloon flight for them. No one was sure yet if the air above the earth was safe for living things to breathe. So for their command performance, the brothers tied a basket to the floating bag and sent up a duck, a rooster, and a sheep. The animals survived, and it was established that air from the atmosphere was safe to breathe.

Even though the animals lived through the flight, it was still not certain that the upper air was entirely suitable for humans. So when the Montgolfiers made plans to launch the first human flight in a balloon about two months later, on November 21, 1783, someone suggested that a prisoner should be the first person to go up. But a young French physician, Jean-François Pilatre de Rozier, seized upon this opportunity to fly. He and another Frenchman, the Marquis d'Arlandes, volunteered, and they became the first humans to fly using a balloon. Their flight was a twenty-five minute, five-mile adventure over the rooftops of Paris. D'Arlandes carried a wet sponge to extinguish any fires that might start in the fabric of the balloon.

At about the same time, another Frenchman, Jacques Charles, had begun experimenting with balloons filled with hydrogen. Hydrogen is the lighter-than-air gas that was discovered by Sir Henry Cavendish less than twenty years earlier. Just ten days after de Rozier's first hot-air balloon flight, Charles made a successful two-hour flight, also over Paris, using one of his hydrogen-filled balloons.

Whether filled with hydrogen or hot air, the first balloon flights were sensational. Crowds of excited people gathered underneath and followed the balloons wherever the wind carried them. But as balloon flights continued over the next fifty years, people gradually became bored with them. In the United States, for instance, Professor Charles Durant was mentioned only briefly in the local newspapers when he made a series of balloon flights around Baltimore from 1830 to 1834. Balloons were being taken for granted by some people. Others were working to improve them.

The Father of Aerodynamics

A boy of ten when the first balloon flights were made in France, Sir George Cayley was fascinated throughout his life by the idea of flying. But Cayley had many other diverse interests, too. He was a member of the British Parliament, an engineer, and an inventor who experimented with hot-air engines and artificial human limbs. But Cayley was most interested in the possibility of a flying machine. Unlike the balloons which floated through the air, his flying machine would be a powered vehicle that could be flown from place to place. It would require a stable, fixed wing that Cayley theorized would catch the wind and help lift the craft into the air. With a source of power to propel it, such a machine would give the pilot more control than balloonists had. Balloonists could go only up or down, and they were at the mercy of the wind.

Like da Vinci, Cayley studied closely the flight of birds and thought about constructing a machine with a similar shape. By 1810, he designed several gliders. His designs followed the principles of hydrodynamics, the study of the

Sir George Cayley pioneered the science of aerodynamics and formulated important airplane design principles. He designed the first flying machine with fixed wings and control surfaces on the tail.

motion of fluids, discovered by Swiss mathematician Daniel Bernoulli in 1738. Bernoulli's principle states that the higher the speed of a flowing liquid, the lower the pressure exerted by the substance. In other words, the faster a liquid flows, the less it pushes against things around it. Cayley applied Bernoulli's principle to air and thus es-

In 1853, Sir George Cayley built this glider model. After designing many models, Cayley built the first man-carrying glider.

HOW A CURVED WING CREATES LIFT

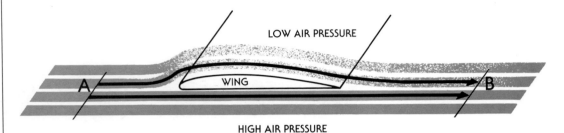

LOW AIR PRESSURE

A

WING

B

HIGH AIR PRESSURE

The curved surface along the top of an airplane's wing forces the air to travel faster above the wing than below it. As shown here, both the air going over the wing and the air going under it travel from A to B in the same amount of time. But the air above the wing has farther to travel because of the curve, so it must move faster than the air below the wing.

The faster air moves, the less pressure it exerts per square inch. Therefore, the air pressure beneath the wing is greater than the air pressure above it. This extra pressure pushes, or lifts, the plane into the air.

tablished the science of aerodynamics, the study of gases in motion. Cayley discovered that he could create a lifting force based on the speed of an air flow. He decided that he would build a wing with a curved upper surface and a bottom surface that was almost flat. With that shape, the speed of the air on top of the wing is greater than the speed of the air below. The pressure of the air below the wing is also greater than the pressure on the top surface. Therefore, the movement of the air exerts an upward force on the wing, which is known as lift.

Putting this force to use, Cayley persuaded his carriage driver to operate one of his curved-wing gliders in 1854. Glider and man became airborne for a few seconds. Cayley was delighted with the results, but his carriage driver was not. Upon landing, he immediately quit his job.

Although he had achieved success with gliders, Cayley knew that a light-

weight source of power would be required for controlled, sustained flight. The only reliable power source in the first half of the eighteenth century was the steam engine, which used large, heavy boilers. Cayley knew it would be impossible for a machine to fly while carrying such a heavy and unwieldy engine. This led him to speculate about the possibility of the sudden combustion of flammable powders or liquids as a source of power. Perhaps a vehicle could be propelled by the explosive but controlled force of burning fuels, he thought. In effect, Cayley foresaw the internal-combustion engine long before it existed. This engine eventually became the driving force for all sorts of vehicles, from lawn mowers to motorboats, cars, and airplanes.

Even though he never found the power source he needed, Cayley continued working with gliders and made more glider flights before he died in

1857. His work earned him the title "the father of aerodynamics."

One of Cayley's followers was William Henson, who received a patent from the British government in 1843 for his "aerial steam carriage." With a design based upon Cayley's work, on paper it looked very much like the airplanes that finally flew sixty-five years later. Henson's machine was never built, however. Like Cayley, Henson realized that the weight of a steam engine would make his plane too heavy to fly. He scaled down his plans and in 1848 tried to fly a smaller model of the steam carriage, powered by a relatively small steam engine. The engine, however, did not generate enough power to propel the craft. Without the needed propulsion, the powered aircraft was successful only at gliding.

The work of Cayley and Henson showed that a smaller and more efficient power source was needed. In 1871, another inventor tried a different approach on a smaller scale. Frenchman Alphonse Penaud designed a stable twenty-inch glider, powered by a rubber band.

Called a "planophere," the tiny flying machine actually worked. Penaud

William Henson designed this aerial steam carriage. Although it was never built, its design closely resembled the first successful airplanes.

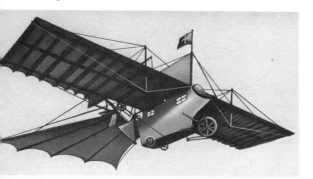

was well ahead of his time. His plane's curved wing tips and tail pattern were similar to those on airplanes of the future. The planophere was manufactured as a toy, but Penaud considered his invention more than a plaything. He thought his basic plan for a flying machine was a sound idea. So he designed a full-size craft that included retractable landing gear and a single control for all flight operations. But Penaud could not get financial backing, and the plane was never built.

Penaud's toy, however, did make an important contribution to the future of flight. Far from France in a small town in Iowa, the planophere provided inspiration to the two young Wright brothers. They were delighted when their father brought one home for them to play with. They soon wore it out, in fact. They tried to build their own, but it would not fly.

Another early experimenter was Britain's Sir Hiram Maxim, inventor of the machine-gun. He built a huge aircraft with a wingspan of 104 feet. Powered by two steam engines, it weighed 3 1/2 tons. The steam engines were able to generate enough power to just barely lift the machine off the railroad tracks that supported it. But it never truly flew. Getting it off the ground was enough for Maxim, however, and he never tried to improve upon the huge machine.

Skeptics Add to the Challenge

Small successes like the planophere and Maxim's heavy machine gradually increased the understanding of aerodynamics. These attempts also motivated other experimenters to keep trying new ways of achieving flight. It provided a tremendous challenge, like a difficult puzzle to be put together. If the puzzle ever were solved, there would also be practical benefits. This did not occur to most people, however. People generally figured that attempts to fly were a waste of time. Even if the crazy people who were trying to fly ever did succeed, what good would it do? Most people thought it would be useless.

People did not consider that airplanes might someday shorten travel time dramatically. For most of the 1800s, they could travel only by horse, steamship, or train. Automobiles were not available until around 1900. If a traveler's destination were not a city connected by rail, the person faced a long and difficult journey. In these cases, travelers went on horseback, in a horse-drawn buggy, by ship, or by a combination of these methods.

Also, it did not occur to most people that airplanes would be able to deliver mail and goods much faster than ever before possible. Until the 1860s, mail was delivered by train, very slowly. In the early 1860s, the pony express was introduced. This service used a relay system of riders and horses and could transport a letter across the country in eight days. This was still much longer than it would take an airplane.

Otto Lilienthal's Contribution

Despite the fact that even well-known, intelligent people considered human flight an idea without merit, some people kept trying. By the early 1890s, there was still no lightweight source of power.

Nor was there a reliable means of control for aircraft. Lacking these essentials, Otto Lilienthal in Germany focused his attention on advancing the development of gliders. Lilienthal was a skilled engineer who designed gliders based upon his detailed studies of the flight of birds. He also used his engineering expertise to build a special hill, where he would run down the slope and jump into the air with his winged glider.

Lilienthal made many flights off his homemade hill. He found that by shifting his weight during flight, he could control the direction of the glider. He began making his flights just as newspapers were developing the technology to publish photographs. Photographers caught Lilienthal in action, soaring through the air on his glider like a bird. The photos were published in newspapers around the world. They inspired many, including the Wrights, to think more seriously about the possibility of human flight.

Lilienthal made more than two thousand glider flights and advanced the science of aviation more than anyone before him. He also reminded people why they were afraid of falling. He died after breaking his back in a glider crash in 1896.

Professor Langley's Aerodrome

By the turn of the century, Professor Samuel B. Langley, an astronomer and director of the Smithsonian Institution in Washington, D.C., was convinced that a powered flying machine was possible. A well-respected scientist, Langley designed the aerodrome. This glider included all the features of the most successful gliders up to that point. He also gave the aerodrome a new gasoline powered engine, designed by Charles Manly, an engineer.

The pair had some success operating a small, unpiloted model of the aerodrome over the Potomac River. So in the fall of 1903, they decided to try a flight with Manly as the pilot. They launched the aerodrome using a specially built catapult on a boat in the Potomac. The launching gear did not work properly, however, and the plane went nose-down into the river. Manly climbed out of the water cold and wet but unhurt. Langley and Manly tried again two months later, but this attempt also failed. This time the aerodrome was badly damaged. Manly survived again but decided to quit trying to fly before he hurt himself seriously.

Langley's failed attempts at flight had an unfortunate side effect. Many people decided that if the Smithsonian Institution's own Professor Langley could not build a successful flying machine, then nobody could.

Chanute Sets the Stage

Langley's failure, however, did not stop Octave Chanute. An American civil engineer, he too felt certain that a powered airplane would soon be a reality. Chanute had been a student of flight since 1875. He published the first real history of aviation, *Progress in Flying Machines,* in 1894. He also kept in contact with aviation researchers throughout Europe and the United States. His knowledge later made him a valuable consultant to the Wright brothers, who would ask him for his opinions on their gliders.

German-born Otto Lilienthal takes off and soars above the ground in his glider. Lilienthal was the first to use curved wings in the development of his gliders.

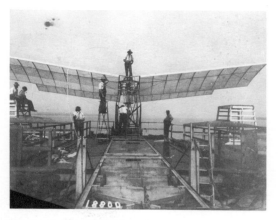

Professor Samuel B. Langley of the Smithsonian Institution built this powered glider called the aerodrome. Langley abandoned the aerodrome because it failed to sustain piloted flight.

In the development of this glider model, Octave Chanute created movable wings that were used to control the glider.

Chanute provided aviation information to anyone who wanted it. He also made his own significant contributions to the emerging science. He felt that "movable surfaces" on an aircraft, such as wings that could be tilted, were a better means of control than Lilienthal's method of shifting the pilot's weight. In 1896, Chanute took Lilienthal's basic design and added movable wings and a

Octave Chanute, U.S. engineer and aviator, discovered many principles of aerodynamics. In 1894, he published the first book about the history of flight.

metal framework called trusses to strengthen and stabilize his own glider. This improved glider was not a machine capable of controlled, sustained flight, but it was one step closer.

The idea of human flight had to be a powerful dream to survive for thousands of years. It frightened many people, and it seemed ridiculous to others. But it remained an attractive idea for some people. Those who tried to fly were often told it was impossible, but they persisted in trying. When they succeeded, however, they were heroes. The Montgolfiers, Alphonse Penaud, and Otto Lilienthal were unable to build powered, full-size, controllable flying machines, but they all succeeded in freeing the imaginations of earthbound people.

The earliest pioneers of aviation also left a growing body of information for two brothers, who now lived in Dayton, Ohio, who were interested in flight. Wilbur and Orville Wright were inquisitive and inventive. Working as a team, they had built a successful business selling bicycles. In 1900, they turned their full attention to the dream of human flight.

Miracle at Kitty Hawk

There was little in their background to suggest that the Wright brothers would change the world forever. Sons of a bishop in the United Brethren Church in Dayton, Ohio, Orville (born in 1867) and Wilbur Wright (born in 1871) grew up as normal boys. Like others their age, they went ice skating in the winter and flew kites in the spring. But with their two older brothers and a younger sister, Wilbur and Orville shared a powerful family trait:

The young Wright brothers' family takes a drive.

U.S. aviators Orville and Wilbur Wright spent many hours discussing flight. They built the first successful heavier-than-air powered airplane.

all of the Wrights were curious and inventive, and they always wanted to know how things worked.

Wilbur was thirteen and Orville nine when their father gave them a planophere, one of the rubber band-powered toys designed by Alphonse Penaud. Naturally, the young Wright brothers took it apart to see how it worked, then tried to build their own planophere. Like Penaud, they reasoned that a larger model of the toy would fly even better than the small plaything. When they found that this was not true, they lost interest in it.

The brothers had other ambitious hobbies to pursue, such as publishing a small newspaper. They also built and

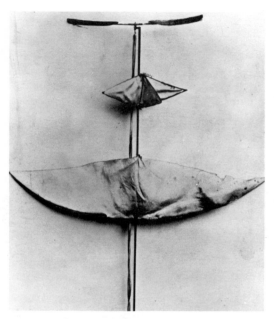

This toy airplane, called a planophere, is powered by rubber bands. It aroused the young Wright brothers' interest in flight.

Awakened by Lilienthal's Crash

The event that focused their attention on the idea of flight was Otto Lilienthal's fatal crash in 1896. Orville and Wilbur began thinking together about the possibility of constructing a flying machine, as they had before when they received the toy planophere. Hungry for information on human flight, they checked the Dayton library but found little. They knew from reading the newspapers, however, that Professor Samuel Langley of the Smithsonian Institution was researching the subject. So they sent a letter requesting copies of any publications the Institution had regarding human flight. As soon as they received the information, they went to work.

Orville later wrote:

On reading the different books on the subject we were much impressed with the great number of people who had given thought to it—among these some of the greatest minds the world has produced. After reading the pamphlets sent to us by the Smithsonian we became highly enthusiastic with the idea of gliding as a sport. We found that Lilienthal had been killed through his inability to properly balance his machine in the air . . . . Chanute, and I believe all the other experimenters before 1900, used the same method of maintaining the equilibrium [balance] in gliding flight. We at once set to work to devise a more efficient means of maintaining the equilibrium.

What was needed, the Wrights observed, was a mechanical way to balance the glider while it was in flight. Before long they had formed an idea: if

sold kites. They were always handy with tools, and when they grew into young men, they opened a bicycle shop. The Wrights enjoyed the creative work of designing new and better bicycles. They were both good craftsmen, and they were also good at thinking out design problems. But once they mastered the problem of design, building the bicycles seemed tedious work.

With the bike shop well-established, the hard-working brothers needed a new challenge. It would have to capture their interest in mechanics and engineering. It would also have to be something that they could feel passionate about. To attract their interest, a new challenge would have to pique their curiosity, fill them with wonder, and give them a new world of ideas to explore. In other words, it had to be something that was impossible. For the otherwise law-abiding Wrights, the law of gravity became the perfect challenge.

they could make the front part of one wing turn upward when the other wing was turned downward, they could use the flow of air around it to stabilize the glider. Manipulating the wings in a certain way, they reasoned, would keep the glider balanced and in flight. The pilot would not have to shift his own weight around, as Lilienthal and others had done with disastrous results.

With that idea well-formed, the next step was to design the craft. It had to be flexible enough to allow for such a wing-bending design yet strong enough to carry a pilot. Wilbur came up with a possible solution to the problem one day in the bike shop. He sold an inner tube to a customer and suddenly noticed something interesting about the cardboard box that had held the tube. He saw how the opposing surfaces of the box could be made to curve in opposite directions by pinching and twisting the box in a certain way.

The effect on the box was just what Wilbur and Orville had envisioned for their glider. Wilbur brought the cardboard box home that evening and explained his idea to Orville. They thought some more about it, then decided to write to glider expert Octave Chanute. Chanute was then the most dedicated and experienced flight experimenter in the world. He would surely have an opinion.

That first letter was the beginning of a ten-year relationship. During this relationship, the Wrights often benefitted from Chanute's expertise in aeronautics, the science of aircraft operation. For his part, Chanute was delighted to find these two brothers who were so serious and diligent about the idea of flight.

Studying Lilienthal's Results

The brothers continued their research. They studied Lilienthal's observations of birds, which explained the principle of lift. Lilienthal's research illustrated that pigeons, for instance, use quick strokes of their short, heavy wings to propel themselves into flight. Other birds, like sea gulls, use the slower flapping motion of their long, narrow wings for gliding. All species of birds rely upon the wind as a lifting force. This knowledge reinforced the Wrights' belief that the key to achieving flight was a matter of controlling the wings of the aircraft as they met the wind.

By 1897, the Wrights were getting ready to test their radically different ideas. They designed a glider similar to Lilienthal's but with a major innovation. Their glider would have a system of pulleys and cables that would allow them to bend the wings during flight. The glider's frame was made of lightweight wooden poles of spruce and ash. Unbleached muslin was stretched over the frame to form the wings.

The Wrights' glider is being flown as a kite to test wing strength. The brothers' early work with gliders was influenced by the experiments of Otto Lilienthal.

WING WARPING

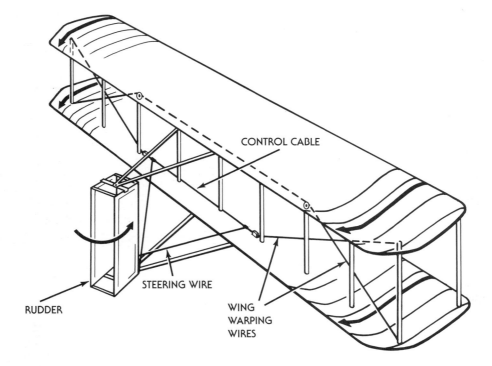

CONTROL CABLE

RUDDER

STEERING WIRE

WING
WARPING
WIRES

The Wright brothers devised their wing warping system so that planes could turn more smoothly. On their plane, the rudder, which controls the direction the plane turns, was connected by wires to a control cable, which is what the pilot used to steer the plane. Also attached to the control cable, however, were wires that ran to the rear corners of each wing. Whenever the pilot moved the control cable to turn the plane, the cable also pulled these wires, which "warped" the shape of the wing. When the pilot turned to the right, for example, the wing corners on the right side of the plane were tipped up, and the corners on the left side were tipped down. This would cause the plane to bank, or tip, slightly to the right as it turned. Airplanes today still use this principle of wing warping, but it is accomplished with steel flaps, or ailerons, on the wings.

One of the frustrations of piloting a glider was dealing with the ever-changing speed and direction of the wind. With wings that could be bent during flight, the pilot would be able to react to sudden gusts and reposition the wings to avoid crashing. Wilbur and Orville called their new idea "wing-warping."

The Wrights began searching for the ideal spot to test their controllable wings. They needed a place with steady, high winds and wide, open spaces. Again, they wrote to Washington, D.C., this time for government weather records. They found that the perfect place to launch their test glider would be on the breezy beach near Kitty Hawk, North Carolina. The location was remote, barren, and windy, which was the most important condition.

In August 1899, Wilbur took the train from Dayton to Virginia. He then hired a sailor to take him on to Kitty Hawk. Wilbur carried with him the Wright brothers' unassembled, first aircraft, a kite with two five-foot wings. Wilbur began setting up camp when he arrived, and Orville joined him a few weeks later.

Wing-Warping Put to the Test

Living out of a tent at the wind-blown beach, Wilbur and Orville put together their kite, tied it to a stake, and flew it. It was not meant to carry a pilot but to test the wing-warping system the brothers had devised. They tried different wing shapes and observed how these shapes affected the performance of the

The Wright brothers test their glider's newly developed wing-warping system. They discovered that they could maneuver the aircraft by controlling the shape and angle of the wings.

kite. They found that by designing the leading edge of their wing to curve into the wind and then taper off, they were able to create a lifting force beneath the wing. With their system of pulleys, they could control the strength of the lift. They gained confidence that they were on the right course and returned to Dayton for the winter.

Although they had not yet even attempted a human flight, the Wrights made some important findings during that first trip to Kitty Hawk. They discovered that Lilienthal's calculations regarding lift were wrong. In order to find the correct figures, the Wrights built a small wind tunnel in their bike shop. There they tested many wing models of different shapes to see how each would react to the air moving around it.

They made their wind tunnel by placing a small fan at one end of a tin cylinder. At the opposite end, they

In 1901, the Wright brothers built this wind tunnel, which enabled them to observe the interaction of moving air and various wing shapes. Using this information, they refined their glider model.

hung small pieces of tin and wax, in various shapes, resembling the design of wings. The brothers found that the greatest lifting effect occurred when the winglike shapes were curved a certain way into the wind. This confirmed what they had learned with their kite at Kitty Hawk. They recorded the exact angles at which the greatest and least lift occurred. They would use this new information to design their next glider.

The wind tunnel tests proved that much of the available data regarding flight were probably incorrect—just as Lilienthal's calculations were. The Wrights became concerned about wasting their time following other false leads. They were skeptical about any information or theories that they had not developed and proved themselves.

The First Kitty Hawk Glider

After another summer in the bike shop, Wilbur and Orville returned to Kitty Hawk in October 1900 with a full-size glider. It was "a tailless biplane with a horizontal control surface forward of the wings." The odd-shaped craft was similar to a glider previously designed by Chanute, who had been an early proponent of wing control. But again, the important difference in the Wrights' design was their wing-warping system. One wing of the glider could be tipped up while the other one was tipped down.

Finally, the Wrights would be able to put their theories about wing control to the test with a full-fledged glider that could hold a pilot. After sleeping in a tent the previous year, they decided to construct two buildings. One was to house their glider, and one was for

them to live in. They settled in and waited for a day when the wind was right. Then they carried the glider up to a big sand dune near their camp.

Wilbur and Orville successfully made about a dozen flights. One brother would lie down on the glider. The other would hold onto a wing and run the glider downhill into the wind until it began soaring by itself. The first few flights lasted only about five to ten seconds. Eventually, however, they were able to keep the glider in the air for twenty seconds, about a foot or two off the ground.

The results were less than spectacular. In all of their flights combined, the Wrights spent a total of only about two minutes up in the air. It was much less time than they had hoped, and it could hardly be called human flight. But when they went back to Dayton, the Wrights were not discouraged. Wilbur later wrote that although the many hours they had hoped to practice dwindled down to a few minutes, they were

The Wright brothers designed, constructed, and housed their aircraft in this factory at Kitty Hawk, North Carolina.

still pleased. Using an unproved design based upon radical ideas, Wilbur concluded they had done fairly well: "We considered it quite a point to be able to return without having our pet theories completely knocked in the head by the hard logic of experience, and our brains dashed out in the bargain."

A New Theory of Flight

Attempting human flight was certainly a dangerous business. The Wright brothers knew well that Lilienthal and many others had died trying to fly. Unlike the others, the Wrights were concerned with the issue of controlling the aircraft once it was in the air. Experimenters before them had presumed that it might be steered much like a ship in the water.

Wilbur and Orville's glider experiments were proving that this was not true. Controlling the aircraft depended on many factors, including how the structure was shaped and how it moved in the wind. By focusing on the problem of control, the Wright brothers were building upon the science of aerodynamics that Cayley had discovered and to which others had contributed. Questioning and refining the old theories, and adding their own carefully tested findings, the Wrights were developing a well-formed theory of flight.

The curved shape of their wing would divide the air passing around it, the Wrights reasoned. Air passing above the wing would move faster than air passing below it. Applying Bernoulli's principle, they concluded that fast-moving air would exert less pressure than slow-moving air. Therefore, the greater pressure below the wing would push it

upward, creating a force called lift. The Wrights theorized that when lift was perfectly balanced with the weight of the aircraft, flight would result.

To balance the force of the lift with the weight of the aircraft, the Wrights had to find the center of gravity in the aircraft. They had to be able to keep the center of gravity stable and rotate the aircraft around it in order to keep it balanced. The center of gravity, they found, lies between the wings. To stabilize and balance the aircraft around that center, they had to be able to change the way the wings met the wind.

Until it is perfectly balanced there are three different ways that an aircraft will rotate in the air. The way that the craft rotates depends on how the pilot maneuvers three sets of movable surfaces. These are the steering mechanisms used to keep the aircraft under control. These steering mechanisms have continued to evolve since the Wrights' day.

The Wright brothers test their glider during one of their many experiments. They learned important methods of aircraft control during these flights.

AN AIRPLANE'S THREE BASIC MOVEMENTS

PITCH	YAW	ROLL

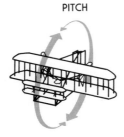

Pitch occurs when the front of an airplane moves up or down.

Yaw describes the swinging of a plane from side to side.

Roll is what happens when the wings of the plane dip to one side or the other.

The three types of movement are called pitch, yaw, and roll. Pitch occurs when the nose of the aircraft goes down and the tail goes up. Pitch is controlled by steering devices called elevators. If the craft continues pitching, it will turn end over end. Yaw describes what happens when the aircraft turns on a horizontal axis. Horizontal movement is controlled by the rudder. If the plane continues to yaw, the entire aircraft will spin like a record on a turntable. Roll happens when the aircraft's wings turn in a spiral. A movable part of an airplane wing called an aileron controls this sort of motion. If the aircraft continues rolling, its wings will move in the way that a football spins when thrown in a spiral.

The actions of the elevators, the rudder, and the ailerons must be carefully coordinated. Used in combination, these mechanisms control the equilibrium of the aircraft and keep the plane from tumbling out of control.

Of course, the Wrights did not know all the details of plane move-ment yet, but they were learning fast. They returned to Kitty Hawk with a new glider again in 1901 and with another one in 1902. They encountered many frustrations, including monsoon-like weather conditions and unbearable mosquitoes. But they kept trying, living and working out of their wooden cabin at the beach.

The Breakthrough: A Glider with Thrust

When the weather permitted, the Wrights flew their glider enthusias-tically. They gradually became expert glider pilots, building the skills they would need later when they attempted powered flight. After they made more than one thousand glider flights during a period of three years, the Wrights felt certain that they could build a powered machine that would fly. With their in-novative wind-warping idea, they had solved the problem of lift. Now they had only to figure out how to provide

In 1903, the Wright brothers built the Wright Flyer I, *the first powered aircraft with propellers and a gasoline engine.*

the necessary thrust to power their glider through the air.

Beginning in February 1903, the Wrights began gathering the best materials, including wood and fabric, they could find for constructing a powered flying machine, the *Wright Flyer I*. They decided that the thrust would be provided by propellers, powered by a twelve-horsepower gasoline engine. The engine was designed by the Wrights and built by Charlie Taylor, a skillful mechanic they had hired to work in the bicycle shop. Taylor's engine would use a chain and sprocket design, similar to the bicycle design that the Wrights were so familiar with.

This propeller creates forward motion, called thrust, in the Wrights' airplane.

The brothers had debated for many hours what the proper design of the propellers should be. Exactly what would be the perfect shape? How should the propellers be mounted? How fast should they spin and in what direction? These were difficult questions that no one had ever answered.

The Wrights had a peculiar way of debating such questions. They often discussed matters of aerodynamics after dinner in their house in Dayton. From the kitchen, their sister Katherine could hear them arguing in the living room. Their voices would grow louder as Wilbur and Orville voiced their disagreements on some point of aircraft design. But often a funny thing happened.

After arguing back and forth for a while, the brothers would suddenly realize that they had switched positions. Wilbur would be supporting Orville's original point, and vice versa. They found that with mutual respect and a lack of stubbornness, they often arrived at the same point of view. This method also allowed each brother to see both sides of a problem and gain a larger

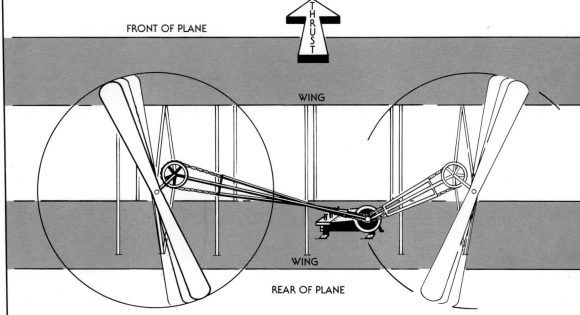

PROPELLERS DRIVEN BY CHAIN AND SPROCKET

THRUST

FRONT OF PLANE

WING

WING

REAR OF PLANE

To provide the thrust for their airplane, the Wright brothers attached two propellers to the rear of the wings. Each of the propellers was attached to a chain and sprocket assembly just like the chain and sprocket on a bicycle. A small gas-powered engine turned the chains, which spun the propellers. The air movement produced by the spinning propellers pushed the plane forward.

perspective on questions of aircraft design. It was almost as if the problem of flight were too difficult for one person alone.

Working as a team through the summer months, the Wrights were ready to return to Kitty Hawk by late September 1903. They brought with them the *Wright Flyer I*. They were eager to try the new craft out. But soon after they arrived, a powerful storm hit, buffeting their wooden cabin with winds up to seventy miles per hour. Six inches of rainwater covered the floor by the time the storm stopped four days later.

They cleaned up the camp, thankful that the unassembled pieces of the flyer survived the storm undamaged.

They eagerly put the flyer together. When they started up the motor, however, it backfired violently, causing the entire plane to shake. The engine worked, but it turned the chain and sprockets unevenly. The sprockets were attached to tubular shafts that would spin the propellers. As they began spinning with the sprockets, one of these propeller shafts became badly twisted. The plane would not fly like this. The Wrights knew there was only one thing to do: send it back to Ohio. In Dayton, their helper Charlie Taylor would reinforce both propeller shafts. This work would cause a lengthy delay, but it had to be done. By mid-November, the propeller shafts had been strengthened and were ready to put back on the flyer.

Home by Christmas?

The brothers were stalled again, however. Kitty Hawk was struck with more bad weather through Thanksgiving, including some snow. The weather finally cleared near the end of the month, and the Wrights brought the flyer back out. But while running the engine, they noticed another problem with the tubular propeller shafts. This time one had cracked. It seemed that their hoped-for flight would not happen by Christmas.

Again the Wrights made a quick decision. Orville traveled back to Dayton and had Charlie Taylor construct solid propeller shafts of high-grade steel. Taylor worked quickly, and Orville was back at Kitty Hawk by December 9.

Three days later, the improved shafts were in place.

With their mechanical troubles finally solved, the Wrights were eager to try the flyer out the next day. But they needed a certain amount of wind to produce the required lift, and it was just not windy enough. Although the wind picked up the following day, it was Sunday and the Wrights never worked on Sunday. On Monday, December 14, the wind had died down again. But Wilbur and Orville were determined to make a flight, with or without the wind. They had promised that they would be home for Christmas, and time was running out.

Before attempting their first flight, they ran up a flag on a makeshift flagpole to alert the local lifeguards and people on the beach. Five men, two boys, and a dog came to watch. Wilbur won the coin toss to see who would go first. He climbed on, lying down on his stomach. Orville spun the propellers to get the engine started. He then ran alongside, guiding the machine along the sixty-foot wooden runner they had

The Wright Flyer I *is flown at Kitty Hawk on December 17, 1903, marking the dawn of a new era in history.*

placed in the sand. Orville also carried a stopwatch, which he started as soon as the flyer left the ground.

At the controls, Wilbur turned the rudder as soon as the plane left the track. The plane immediately went upward, then came down on its tail, damaging one of the wings. It had traveled only about one hundred feet, and the flight was over in less than four seconds. It was not really a flight, but the brothers were still very excited. They had learned that their design was fundamentally correct, and success could not be far off.

The damage to the flyer was slight, and the brothers immediately set about fixing it. A few days later, Orville got his chance to fly. At 10:35 A.M. on December 17, 1903, he climbed onto the flyer. With Wilbur steadying the wing, Orville steered the flyer down the track and took off into the air. His flight lasted a little longer than Wilbur's, a total of about twelve seconds, but he landed the flyer without damage after he went about 120 feet. As soon as it was over, they brought the plane back to the launching pad and tried again. In the next ninety minutes, they made three more flights, with the brothers alternating at the controls. Wilbur made the final flight of the day, covering 852 feet and staying up for fifty-nine seconds.

The Wright brothers dramatically changed the course of human history that day. It was the first time a heavier-than-air vehicle had left the earth under its own power, accomplished controlled and sustained flight, then landed at a spot as high as the spot it had taken off from. A new age had begun, although no one realized it. "At the time we flew our first power plane we were not thinking of any practical uses at all," Orville said years later. "We just wanted to show that it was possible to fly."

Practical uses would come later. First, the Wrights had to reverse a fundamental assumption about the limits of humankind. "If people were meant to fly, they would have wings"—this was the popular slogan of skeptics. The Wrights proved them wrong. They showed that by using their brains and the resources around them, people could extend their abilities as far as they could imagine. They could even do what most people thought impossible.

The Wrights' progress was not easy. They had worked together, challenging old assumptions and arguing until they changed each other's opinions. They cared little for what people thought. When they were done, the two brothers had amended what was until then an agreed-upon law of the universe. Newton was still right: what goes up must come down. But not right away. The force of gravity could be overcome, at least temporarily.

More so than anyone before them, the Wrights had looked at human flight as a scientific problem to be solved. First, they learned all they could about the subject. Then, they persisted when things became difficult. Their ultimate success was not an accidental discovery or the result of luck. It took several years of rigorous thinking and patient, hard work. Perhaps most of all, it required faith in a dream.

Someone once asked Orville at what point he got the biggest kick out of flying: was it when that first flight left the ground? "No," he said. "I got more thrill out of flying before I had ever been in the air at all—while lying in bed thinking how exciting it would be to fly."

A New Age Takes Wing

The Wrights did, in fact, make it home in time for Christmas in 1903. They received no heroes' welcome, since Wilbur and Orville chose to keep their triumph quiet. They shared the news of their flight with their family and a few close friends like Octave Chanute, but generally they did not try to publicize their success. The brothers hoped to obtain a patent on their design, so they were not eager to have others find out about it and quickly copy it. They knew that their flying machine would be valuable, and they hoped to sell the design to the U.S. and British governments.

When the Wrights wrote letters, however, describing the *Wright Flyer I* to the U.S. Army, they were dismissed as crackpots. The prevailing attitude toward flight was still one of great skepticism. Perhaps the world was not yet ready for their flying machine. In the meantime, however, the brothers worked at making their flying machine ready for the world.

The *Wright Flyer II* came out in 1904, and the *Wright Flyer III* in 1905. Instead of making the difficult trip back to Kitty Hawk, the Wrights regularly flew these planes at Huffman Prairie, about eight miles from their home in Dayton. They made more than forty flights in 1905, the longest of which covered a distance of thirty-four miles. They gradually learned the skills necessary to maneuver the aircraft. Soon, they were able to fly complete circles over the prairie.

Around Dayton, word gradually spread that the Wrights had made a successful flying machine. It was an incredible piece of news. Yet no one seemed to appreciate what the brothers had done. The fact of a flying machine was probably just too unbelievable for people to accept. Also, there was confu-

The Wright brothers were inspired by their initial success with powered flight. In 1904, they built the Wright Flyer II, *shown here being flown in a field near their home in Dayton.*

At Fort Myer, Virginia, U.S. army officials and civilian spectators watch as the Wright brothers unload and prepare their airplane for flight.

sion about exactly what the *Wright Flyer* was. It was often called an airship, a term that was also used to refer to dirigibles, the gas-filled balloons that were invented in the 1800s. There was nothing for people to get excited about if it were just another dirigible. Unless they saw the *Wright Flyer* in action, many assumed that it was just that—one of the huge, gas-filled balloons that had been around for more than one hundred years.

It was inevitable that some people would notice the flyer, however. Passengers on a train that ran on nearby tracks reported to the local newspaper that they had seen a machine flying out at Huffman Prairie. The paper sent out a reporter, but the Wrights were not flying that day, and the reporter did not pursue the story any further. But it would be told soon enough.

The Wright brothers are greeted with disbelief by skeptics who assume that the Wright Flyer *is nothing more than a dirigible–a gas-filled balloon.*

(top) *On September 17, 1909, Orville Wright and passenger Thomas Selfridge fly over Fort Myer as thousands of spectators watch.*
(middle) *A propeller breaks, and Orville loses control of the plane.*
(bottom) *Selfridge dies of injuries from the crash. Orville suffered a cut to his head and several broken bones.*

Tragedy Strikes at Fort Myer

By September 1908, the brothers had succeeded in getting the U.S. Army interested enough in their invention to schedule some trial flights at Fort Myer, Virginia. They had also decided to show their invention in Europe, where it might be taken more seriously. While Wilbur was flying one plane in France, Orville flew another at Fort Myer. Orville flew every day that weather allowed, for two weeks. Tens of thousands of people came to Fort Myer to see the spectacle. Millions more read about it in newspapers, where they also saw pictures of Orville in flight.

These exhibition flights ended in tragedy on September 17. That day Orville and his passenger, Lt. Thomas Selfridge, were flying wide circles over a field when one of the plane's propellers broke. As the broken propeller flew into the air, Orville lost control of the plane and crashed. He sustained a broken leg, several broken ribs, and a six-inch cut on his head. Selfridge's injuries were more serious, and he died that night.

Wilbur heard about the accident by telegram in France, where he was demonstrating a plane. Reassured that Orville would be all right, Wilbur stayed in Europe. He felt it was his duty not to disappoint those who had come to see him fly. There was, for instance, a seventy-year-old Frenchman who rode his bicycle sixty miles round-trip every day for almost a week, hoping to witness the miracle of human flight.

Wilbur wrote to his father: "I sometimes get so angry at the continual annoyance of having the crowd about that I feel like quitting the whole thing and going home. But when I think of the sacrifices some of them have made in the hope of seeing a flight, I cannot help feeling sorry for them when I do not go out."

The brothers were international celebrities now, and they felt compelled to show their invention to the world. The next year, when his wounds from the crash had healed, Orville decided it was his turn to show a plane in Europe. Wilbur stayed in the United States. He went to New York and made several flights. More than a million people watched him fly along Manhattan, over the New York Harbor, and around the Statue of Liberty.

Glenn Curtiss's *June Bug*

All this attention did not go unnoticed by other inventors, including Alexander Graham Bell. He had already made his mark on the world by inventing the telephone. Now he organized and financed a small group of people interested in flight, including motorcycle mechanic and racer Glenn Curtiss. Between March and December 1908, this group produced four flying machines, based upon what they knew about the Wrights' design. The first two crashed, but their third airplane, the *June Bug,* was a success. Outfitted with a thirty-horsepower, eight-cylinder, water-cooled engine designed by Curtiss, the *June Bug*'s performance was not as good as the Wrights' planes. But it gave Glenn Curtiss his start, and he would be a competitor of the Wright brothers for years to come.

Europeans were duplicating the Wrights' aeronautical successes, too. In July 1909, Louis Bleriot of France be-

In 1909, Frenchman Louis Bleriot becomes the first person to fly a heavier-than-air machine across the English Channel.

came the first to fly over a large body of water when he made it across the English Channel and collected the prize of ten thousand British pounds offered by the London *Daily Mail.* Bleriot was a wealthy man who financed his flying hobby with money he made from manufacturing headlights for cars. He made the English Channel crossing in the eleventh plane that he had designed and built. It had a twenty-five horsepower, three-cylinder engine and a top speed of thirty-six miles per hour. After his famous flight, Bleriot began manufacturing the plane, making it available to anyone for about two thousand dollars. He also later built more than ten thousand airplanes for the French government during World War I.

The Angle of Attack

From 1908 to 1910, Curtiss, Bleriot, and others pieced together the dynamics of lift and thrust, the crucial secrets of flight that the Wrights had uncov-

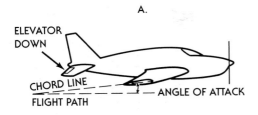

A.

ELEVATOR DOWN

CHORD LINE — ANGLE OF ATTACK

FLIGHT PATH

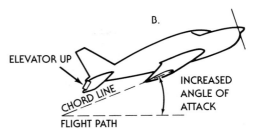

B.

ELEVATOR UP

CHORD LINE

FLIGHT PATH

INCREASED ANGLE OF ATTACK

The angle of attack is the angle formed by a plane's flight path and an imaginary line, called a chord line, that runs at the same angle as the plane's wings. A high angle of attack increases lift, while a low angle of attack decreases it. A pilot decreases the angle of attack by lowering the elevators located on the tail wings (A). The angle of attack can be increased by raising the elevators (B).

ered. As the Wrights had determined earlier, these other pioneers of flight found that the "angle of attack" was a key factor. The angle of attack refers to the position of the wing as the wind hits it. At a low angle of attack, the entire wing is flat and nearly parallel to the ground. When the front part of the wing is tilted upward, more wind rushes underneath it, and the angle of attack is increased.

To get a plane off the ground, the pilot builds up enough speed so that the wind is rushing around the wing. With the correct angle of attack, this creates pressure, or lift, under the wing. The pilot raises the elevator, located in the tail of the plane, and lowers the ailerons, which are on the trailing edge of the wings. These movements of the plane's various surfaces deflect the air flow, increase the angle of attack, and create more lift. The plane leaves the ground when the force of lift becomes greater than the weight of the plane.

Once in the air, the pilot must maintain the balance between lift and gravity. Less lift is required as the plane picks up speed. At high speeds, the pilot may decrease the angle of attack.

Steering the Airplane

The pilot uses the control column and foot pedals to steer the plane. The control column is a stick in the floor of the cockpit. The column is attached to cables that raise and lower the ailerons on the wings and the elevators in the tail.

When the pilot pushes the stick to the right or left, one aileron is raised and the other is lowered. This causes the plane to roll to one side or the other, a necessary movement for smooth banking as the plane turns.

By pushing the stick forward, the pilot lowers the elevators. This diverts the air flow, causing the tail to rise and the nose to drop. As the nose drops,

This aerial exhibition thrills a huge crowd of spectators, who view daring pilots with admiration and respect.

the airplane dives. Pulling back on the stick, the pilot raises the elevators. With the elevators up, the tail drops and the nose rises. As the nose rises, the airplane climbs.

The pilot uses foot pedals to turn the rudder, which diverts wind flow around the tail section and turns the aircraft.

In the first airplanes, these control cables were directly connected from the control column to the movable surfaces. In modern aircraft, the process is computerized. As the pilot moves the control column, signals are sent from the cockpit to hydraulic systems, systems that are operated by the movement of liquid, or electric motors. These then move the surfaces appropriately.

Working the control column and the foot pedals, the pilot carefully orchestrates the action of the plane's movable surfaces to control the aircraft in flight.

To land the plane, the pilot must reduce speed, which reduces lift. But some lift must be created just before touching down to avoid a crash landing. As the pilot glides in to land, he or she increases the angle of attack by gradually raising the elevators and lowering the ailerons on the wings. This creates lift, and the plane lands safely.

The Public Begins to Take Notice

The disbelief and indifference that had first greeted the Wrights' invention of the flying machine were gone by 1910. Everywhere that the Wrights and other flyers went, they were greeted by enthusiastic crowds. The public was beginning to realize that the ancient dream of flight had finally come to life. The impossible had been achieved, and to see it stirred the imagination. In 1910, after a plane flew over the streets of Chicago, a minister who witnessed the event wrote: "Never have I seen such a look of wonder in the faces of a multitude. From the gray-haired man to the child, everyone seemed to feel that it was a new day in their lives."

Airplanes were still too small to carry passengers or freight, so they were not yet very practical. In fact, no one was even certain that airplanes would ever be of any real use. But people were thrilled by the new flying machines, and they would pay to see daring pilots fly. Airplanes became a great source of entertainment. There were exhibitions and aerial meets. The first really large meet occurred in Reims, France, where Glenn Curtiss set a speed record of forty-three miles per hour. Huge crowds would gather at these events to watch the daring pilots push the limits of what was possible.

In addition to the entertainment they provided, airplanes also generated intense competition. All the pilots seemed to want to go faster and farther than anyone else ever had. They demanded better airplanes from the manufacturers, who began providing them. Pilots who flew superior machines were rewarded with prize money, and those manufacturers gained the prestige of producing a winner.

An aerial meet at Boston Harbor in September 1910, for instance, featured more than $100,000 in prize money. The next month, in New York's Belmont Park, Count Jacques de Lesseps of France won $10,000 in a quick flight around the Statue of Liberty; American Ralph Johnstone set a new altitude record of 9,714 feet; and Englishman Claude Graham-White set a new speed record of sixty-one miles per hour.

Also at the Belmont Park meet, the first women pilots appeared, including Helene Dutrieux of France and Americans Blanche Scott and Ruth Law. Within a few years, the Stinson sisters, Katherine and Marjorie, had opened a flying school near San Antonio, Texas. As pilots received more training and became more skillful, new flight records continued to be set.

Record-breaking performances were made for distance as well as speed. Glenn Curtiss's flight of two hours and fifty-one minutes from Albany to New York City in 1910 won him ten thousand dollars from a New York newspaper. The public eagerly followed the

Helene Dutrieux of France appears at an aerial meet at New York's Belmont Park in 1910. Dutrieux was one of the first woman aviators.

accounts of these flights in the newspapers as the prizes became larger and the contests more challenging.

Airplane Pilots as All-American Heroes

Airplanes also provided would-be heroes with the opportunity to prove themselves. Praised for their courage, pilots were admired for exploring the unknown reaches of the sky. They provided real excitement and gave many people a way to extend their imaginations far beyond their ordinary lives. Stories about pilots' daring flights provided people with inspiring thoughts and dreams.

One pilot who gained fame as an adventurous hero was the dashing Calbraith P. Rodgers. In September 1911, the cigar-smoking former college football star took up the challenge laid down by newspaper magnate William Randolph Hearst. Hearst would give fifty thousand dollars to the first pilot to fly from coast to coast in less than thirty days.

Rodgers had received his flight training at a school the Wrights established in Dayton, and he bought a plane made by the Wrights. By this time the Wrights' planes were propelled by piston-powered engines, rather than the chain and sprocket design of the original *Wright Flyer*. Rodgers's flight was sponsored by the Armour Meat Packing Company of Chicago. To capitalize on its aeronautical investment, Armour built an advertising campaign around the event. The company was introducing a new soft drink called Vin Fiz, which also became the name of Rodgers's plane.

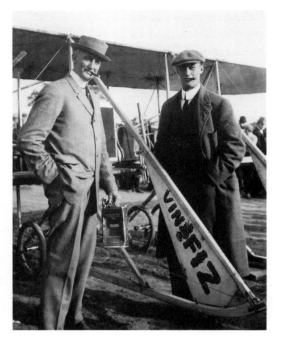

Calbraith Rodgers stands in front of his plane, the Vin Fiz. *The plane was named after a soft drink as an advertising ploy. The name of the product received great exposure during Rodgers's coast-to-coast flight.*

'Vin Fiz, Sold Everywhere, 5 Cents'

For advertisers, Armour's campaign was an exciting new concept. By naming the plane after its product, Armour guaranteed itself plenty of national exposure. Details of the flight would be in every newspaper in the country for at least one month. Additionally, the thousands of people across the country who looked up to see the plane as it went overhead would have no doubt about what soft drink to buy. Painted on the bottom of the plane's wings in huge letters was the name *Vin Fiz*.

Since there was no reliable navigation system for aircraft yet, Rodgers depended upon railroad tracks to guide him across the country. The Armour

Company provided a three-car train that would follow the *Vin Fiz* and provide support. It included a workshop and spare parts, a passenger car for reporters, and a luxurious private Pullman car so that Rodgers's mother and wife could be with the pilot each night. Painted on the side of the train were big purple grapes and a sign that said "Vin Fiz, Sold Everywhere, 5 cents."

Rodgers took off in his airplane from Long Island on a September day. He headed first for Chicago after detouring over Coney Island where he dropped Vin Fiz leaflets along the boardwalk, pioneering another new advertising technique. The first night he stopped in Middletown, New York. As he was taking off the next morning, the rudder of the plane became caught on a tree when Rodgers went low to avoid some power lines, and the *Vin Fiz* slammed into a chicken coop. With a cigar still clenched between his teeth, Rodgers emerged from the wreckage with his head bleeding. Ace airplane mechanic Charlie Taylor, whom Rodgers had hired away from the Wright brothers, had the plane ready to go again in just a few days. But it would not be the last crash of the *Vin Fiz.*

In all, Rodgers had eleven major accidents along the way. Built with more wood than the early *Wright Flyers,* it was a sturdier aircraft, but the plane still had to be almost totally rebuilt four times. The pilot also took a beating, sustaining many injuries, including sprained ankles, a twisted back, a broken leg, a slight concussion, and cuts in his right arm. But the resilient Rodgers was determined to finish what he had started. "Whether I get fifty thousand dollars or fifty cents, I am going to be

In 1911, Calbraith Rodgers flew from Long Island, New York to Long Beach, California, marking the first cross-country flight.

the first to cross the country in an aeroplane," he told reporters.

And he was. Averaging fifty-one miles per hour from one coast to the other, Rodgers finally landed his Wright brothers' plane on the seashore at Long Beach, California, on December 10, 1911. This was forty-nine days after he started. The plane was mobbed by spectators, and he enjoyed a hero's welcome. He had not met Hearst's thirty-day time limit, but as Rodgers said to friends: "I made it, didn't I?"

Like many other early pilots, Rodgers eventually ran out of luck, for flying was truly a dangerous business. Five months after he had landed in triumph, Rodgers was flying low over the surf off Long Beach. He dipped his plane's wings and crashed in shallow water. He did not survive the wreck.

Calbraith Rodgers was not exempt from the dangers of flying. Five months after his famous cross-country flight, he crashed and died in the Vin Fiz.

New Age Begins

The next spring another pioneer of flight died at the age of forty-five after a struggle with typhoid fever. Wilbur Wright's father wrote in his diary: "In memory and intellect, there were none like him. His wit was quick and keen." Before he died, Wilbur Wright had been half of the driving force that ushered in a new age for humankind. The airplane was the most startling invention in the age of invention. It seemed to be a giant step for the human race. The ability to fly would change everything. What might happen next? In the first decade of the new century, it was a major topic of conversation. Much of the discussion was highly optimistic.

For instance, it was argued that because the sky belonged to no one, it was free for anyone to explore, including the poor and oppressed. It was not like land, which went to whoever had enough money to buy. The sky was unclaimed, unregulated, and available to all. With the airplane, it seemed to many people that they would soon be exploring the heavens. They would be like birds—free to go where they wanted, when they wanted. It seemed everyone on the planet would soon become neighbors with everyone else.

Everyone would have an airplane, social observers predicted. People would drive their own personal planes to work every day. Traveling salespeople would hawk their wares from well-stocked airplanes. Airplane racing would become an exciting new sport, rivaling football in its popularity. At the same time, outdoor events like football games would lose money because no one would pay to see them—they would simply watch from above in their airplanes.

These things never happened, of course. Not everyone could afford to own a plane, for one thing. But the fact that people even talked about such possibilities was exhilarating. Before the Wright brothers, any talk of human flight was ridiculed. Afterward, it seemed that because people could fly, anything might be possible. The airplane gave people new hope and new ideas. Thus the airplane had as broad an impact on culture, society, and technology as any other major invention.

A Tool for World Peace?

Decades later, flying would become a routine activity. But in the early 1900s, it was seen as an almost miraculous feat. It seemed that God and the angels in heaven were within reach of the airplanes. Flying was considered a practically divine activity, and some people expected that it would have the effect of making people behave divinely.

Some said that after floating above the clouds, people would rise above all the petty differences that had caused them to go to war in the past. From up in the air, they would gain a new perspective. Borders would be recognized as artificial divisions of one world and would not matter as much as they had in the past. Nations would be closer, in both travel time and in spirit. One of the most talked about ideas of the early 1900s was that the airplane would bring lasting world peace.

It was all speculation, of course, but some people expected that even old enemies would become more neighborly. Relations between the countries of the world would become more peaceful, in part because the airplane offered horrifying new possibilities for destruction. Used as a vehicle to deliver weapons, airplanes would be much more efficient and deadly than the earthbound cannons that had been used in the past. Because of this scenario, many people believed airplanes would serve to deter future wars.

What actually happened was almost the exact opposite. People did use airplanes to fight wars, and the results were more lethal than anyone could have imagined. Eventually, airplanes became very useful tools of death and destruction. But when World War I started in August 1914, there were no specialized military aircraft yet. Soldiers soon discovered, however, that airborne scouts gave them an advantage in tracking the enemy's movements. Of course, the other side began sending up scouting flights, too. At first, pilots on scouting missions would wave when they saw each other up in the sky. But before long, they began packing pistols to ward each other off and to protect their own airplanes. Soon, they were carrying rifles, then machine-guns. As the weaponry became more deadly, greater speed and maneuverability became more important to military aviators.

In 1915, the first real fighter plane appeared. It was the French-made Moraine-Saulnier Bullet. It had one wing, while many other planes at the time had two, one above and one below the fuselage, or body of the plane. It also had a machine-gun mounted on the front, which allowed the pilot to fire straight ahead through the propeller. Wedge-shaped deflectors on the propeller blades protected them from the occasional bullet. The Germans soon produced a plane with a gun driven by the engine. The system was cleverly engineered so that the gun was timed to shoot between the whirling propeller blades. This plane was the Fokker E-1, designed by a young flight engineer named Anthony Fokker. The E-1 made other nations realize they had to produce more heavily armed airplanes in order to defeat enemy aircraft. Through experimentation with horsepower, weight, and dimensions of width and length, scientists made airplanes more efficient in the air.

With better planes and better guns, military pilots would engage each other

The advent of World War I prompted the development of the Moraine-Saulnier Bullet. This French fighter plane is equipped with bullet deflectors and a mounted machine gun.

in combat high above the battle-fields. This one-on-one style of fighting seemed dashing and romantic to some. Pilots became known as "Knights of the Air." Young men who believed the legends and signed on to become fighter pilots found that in reality, fighting in the air was cold, uncomfortable, and deadly.

Changing the Face of War

Soon after World War I started, it was clear that the airplane would forever change the way that armies fought battles. Aerial dogfights and bombing raids were new ways of waging war. New strategies would develop to make the most of the airplane's capabilities, but

This German Fokker E-1 fighter plane was effective in combat because of its efficient artillery system.

there was still much to learn about aviation. In one World War I incident, a commander of the U.S. Army's Ninety-sixth Bombardment Squadron led a six-plane formation over Germany in bad weather and landed on a German airstrip. Because he had no system of navigation, he believed it to be an Allied airfield. The Germans captured the entire squadron and dropped a note on the Ninety-sixth's base that read: "We thank you for the fine airplanes and equipment you have sent us; but what do we do with the major?"

Wartime pilots constantly pushed their airplanes to perform better. Chasing each other across the sky, they developed evasive maneuvers. They learned to fly their planes in loops and rolls as they dodged each other's bullets. Pilots came back from combat flights and told the flight engineers that they needed to be able to go higher, faster, and to turn tighter circles. Others wanted airplanes that could carry bigger payloads of supplies and bombs. Military aviators needed better airplanes, and they got them.

Through continuous refinement of their basic parts, airplanes were steadily improved. Research, design, engineering, and manufacturing functions advanced, and the performance capabilities of airplanes rapidly grew. Heavier, bigger planes with three-hundred horsepower engines, capable of flying at 150 miles per hour, were soon commonplace. Mass production of airplanes and airplane parts began, using some of the assembly line techniques that Henry Ford had pioneered with the automobile. In fact, the Packard Motor Car Company began production of the Liberty engine soon after the United States entered the war. These four-hundred horsepower, twelve-cylinder engines were put into the de Havilland DH-4, a British-designed airplane that was manufactured in the United States by the Dayton-Wright Company. More than twenty-two thousand of these planes were built, but most of them were delivered after the war was over, leaving the U.S. government with a great surplus of airplanes.

World War I is sometimes called "the great accelerator" of aircraft development because of the interest it stimulated in the practical uses of airplanes outside of the military. By the end of the war in November 1918, the average airplane was a much more reliable machine than it had been before. In response to the needs of military pilots, airplanes were produced that were more powerful, better designed, and made with stronger materials. Each new plane was like a new species of bird. They could all fly, but at different speeds and altitudes, depending on the plane's design. When an improvement was made in one plane, it was soon adapted in another. Wings that had been made of canvas were now made from metal, for instance. Engines that had previously required castor oil to keep them lubricated began using better petroleum products. Through trial and error, designers learned more about aerodynamics. They learned that sleek planes flew better, so they made planes with smoother surfaces. The result was that airplanes were faster and more maneuverable than ever.

Flight training had also increased greatly during the war years. By the time the war was over, there were thousands of experienced pilots in the United States alone. These pilots could now fly planes for commercial purposes, such as crop dusting and mail delivery. These uses proved that the airplane was now more than the source of entertainment it had been before the war. Flying remained a highly competitive enterprise, however, as pilots and airplane manufacturers continued to try to set new records for speed, altitude, and distance.

Crossing the Atlantic

In the post-World War I era, new feats of endurance were performed, far exceeding the records that had been set before the war. Airplanes flew over the Atlantic Ocean for the first time in 1919. First, the U.S. Navy's NC-4, designed to float as well as fly, went from Newfoundland in Canada to London, by way of the Azores islands and Lisbon, Portugal, with its crew of six. It took almost fifty-four hours. Later, Englishmen John Alcock and Arthur Whitten Brown flew nonstop from Newfoundland to Ireland in sixteen hours. They collected a prize of 10,000 pounds first offered by the *London Daily Mail* in 1913.

Such feats helped prove that the airplane was a practical means of transport, for both people and things. The U.S. government gave its official stamp of approval in May 1918, when airmail service began between Washington, D.C., and New York. President Warren G. Harding was on hand for a brief ceremony before the historic first flight. But the pilot of that inaugural airmail flight took off the wrong way, and the mail had to be sent back on a train from Maryland.

Despite that embarrassing debut, airmail service between the two cities was a success and was soon expanded to include Chicago and other cities. Some people had argued that the $100,000 the government spent to experiment with the route from Washington to New York was a waste of money. They said that airmail would never work. They were wrong, of course. An especially heroic flight demonstrated that airmail was worth the effort and expense to the nation. In a relay from San Francisco to New York in 1920, mail was delivered coast to coast in 33 hours, compared to 108 hours by train. This was an open-cockpit flight in freezing weather over

Englishmen John Alcock and Arthur Whitten Brown crossed the Atlantic in this airplane. Their record-breaking flight from Newfoundland to Ireland took sixteen hours.

Jack Knight sits in a plane during a mail-delivery mission. Knight's fine performance proved that the airplane is an effective means of moving mail.

the Midwest by Jack Knight. Knight's courage helped convince President Harding that developing an airmail system was in the country's best interests.

Around the World in 174 Days

While some pilots were busy proving the utility of the airplane in practical pursuits, others never stopped looking for bigger challenges. In 1924, four U.S. Army Air Service pilots in two planes took 174 days to fly around the world. The planes were single-engine Douglas World Cruisers. They had a wingspan of fifty feet, four-hundred horsepower engine, and a normal speed of ninety miles per hour. The two-seat Cruisers had open cockpits and were fitted with floats and wheels so that they could touch down on land or in water.

The trip began with four planes, two of which did not make it all the way. They left from Seattle, Washington, on April 6 and went across Alaska, where one of the planes ran

aground in a snowstorm. Another plane made most of the trip but crashed in the Atlantic. Pilots Leigh Wade and Henry Ogden were rescued by a U.S. Navy ship. Pilots Lowell Smith, Leslie Arnold, Erik Nelson, and John Harding made it back to the starting point in Seattle on September 28, 1924, in the remaining two planes, the *Chicago* and the *New Orleans*.

It was an adventurous trip. The four Army Air Service pilots were famous long before the flight was over, and they were mobbed by enthusiastic crowds at every stop. Despite their new status as international heroes, the pilots also had to work as their own mechanics. That part of the job alone kept them busy, since by the end of the trip they had installed nine new engines in each plane.

Their voyage was an accomplishment for all the world to see. The pilots had shown that humans flying airplanes were capable of achieving far beyond what was possible just a few years before. Soaring above the crowds, they had inspired millions, perhaps even some future heroes.

Onward and Upward

People realized by the 1920s that the airplane was more than a curiosity and a source of entertainment. They were also more realistic about the things that might be accomplished with these wonderful flying machines. The early predictions that the airplane would bring world peace were obviously not true. But it was clearly an invention that would change people's lives—perhaps now for the better.

Even with the dramatic advances in airplane performance that came out of World War I, there was still plenty of room for improvement. Small changes were continually made in all aspects of airplane technology. Those changes that made for better performance were incorporated into an airplane's design. An important change was soon copied by other manufacturers. Just as there were coveted prizes for pilots before the war, there were several races in the 1920s and 1930s that also helped spur the development of faster and better airplanes. Speed records continued to be broken as more powerful, efficient engines were developed and stronger, lighter materials were discovered.

The Schneider Trophy was established by Frenchman Jacques Schneider as a reward for outstanding seaplanes. These planes were outfitted with pontoons, or floats, for landing gear so that they could touch down on water. In 1925, Jimmy Doolittle won the Schneider Trophy for flying his Curtiss

Cyrus Bettis poses in front of a powerful R3C-1. Bettis was able to attain a speed of 249 miles per hour in this plane, and thus win the Pulitzer Trophy in 1925.

R3C-2 an average of 235 miles per hour. This was a huge improvement over the best time set in the first great aerial meet, when Glenn Curtiss, whose company made Doolittle's plane, had won with a speed of 43 miles per hour.

Also in 1925, the Pulitzer Trophy was won by Cyrus Bettis, who flew an R3C-1 at an average of 249 miles per hour. This race, for planes that took off and touched down on land, was sponsored by the Pulitzer brothers—Ralph, Joseph, Jr., and Herbert. They owned newspapers in New York and St. Louis and also sponsored prizes for journalists and writers.

These and other contests helped confirm that airplanes were capable of moving people and cargo faster and farther than had ever been imagined, in peacetime as well as war. Contests and races also served to keep the public's attention focused on airplanes and their continuing development. People in business were beginning to realize that airplanes would be a good way to transport relatively small items that had to be moved fast. These included perishable fruits and vegetables and parts needed for repairs.

Still, most people were not involved with or concerned about airplanes on a daily basis. Nor were they aware of the advances being made. But there were some people who were particularly excited about airplanes. They enthusiastically supported efforts to win greater acceptance of airplane use. These people were said to be "air-minded."

The Air-Minded Take to the Skies

Many of the air-minded were able to purchase World War I surplus airplanes, such as the Curtiss JN-4. The JN-4, otherwise affectionately known as the Jenny, could be had for as little as three hundred dollars unused. The no-frills Jenny had a ninety-horsepower, water-cooled engine with eight cylinders. It was capable of a top speed of about seventy-five miles per hour. More than sixty-five hundred Jennies were built. They were used primarily for military training before many of them became barnstorming planes.

Barnstormers enjoyed a life that was carefree, and too often careless. There were still no laws regarding fly-

ing, and no license was required. Anyone with a few hundred dollars could buy a plane and fly anywhere he or she wanted. Many people did just that. Barnstormers traveled from town to town, touching down in cow pastures or open fields. They traveled light, carrying a bedroll so they could sleep under the wing at night. During the day they supported their flying habits by selling rides for a few dollars each.

Besides giving rides, barnstormers thrilled crowds by performing aerial maneuvers and dangerous stunts. They also earned money by providing services like crop dusting. A low-flying plane could rapidly spread pesticide over an entire field, completing in minutes a job that normally took many hours.

A quiet young man from Minnesota, Charles A. Lindbergh, began his aviation career as a barnstormer. He bought a Curtiss Jenny for five hundred dollars, money he had earned performing as a parachutist and wing-walker in Nebraska. Parachutists drew crowds of potential customers for barnstormers, as did wing-walkers. Wing-walkers did stunts while standing on a plane's wing, but they were actually securely strapped to the plane. Like other barnstormers, Lindbergh stopped at fields just outside of small towns or anywhere people would meet. When a group of any size would gather, there were usually a few people who would pay a couple of dollars for an airplane ride.

In this way, barnstormers provided people in many rural areas with their first airplane experiences. These people had read and heard about airplanes and seen pictures of them in newspapers and magazines. But there was nothing like seeing a real flying machine for the first time. It inspired wonder and awe, especially among the isolated people deep in rural areas. Once when he was selling rides in Mississippi, Lindbergh was approached by an elderly woman. He may have thought she was joking when she asked him how much he would charge to fly her to heaven and leave her there. But he soon realized she was entirely serious.

Lindbergh Accepts the Challenge

By 1926, Lindbergh had a different destination in mind. He had decided to accept the challenge presented by Raymond Orteig, a New York restaurateur, who offered twenty-five thousand dollars to anyone who could cross the Atlantic Ocean at its widest point, from New York to Paris. Orteig had first made his offer in 1919, but no one accepted. When he put his challenge up again in 1926, several pilots, including Lindbergh, began preparing for a flight

Daredevil pilots, called barnstormers, search for new ways to thrill audiences. Here, wing-walker Ormer L. Locklear performs stunts as the plane flies over anxious crowds.

across the ocean. It was a dangerous proposition. But Lindbergh knew what he was getting into. He was an able pilot, and he realized that the plane he flew would have to be capable of making the long trip.

Depicted here is a sequence of dramatic feats performed by wing-walkers. Although strapped to the airplane, the wing-walkers are able to move along its body, much to the delight of the crowds below.

A new engine, the Wright J-5 Whirlwind, had recently been introduced. It was a radial, air-cooled engine, which used the movement of the propeller to keep the engine cool rather than the bulky, heavy, water-cooled radiator many other planes were equipped with. The radial engine is an internal-combustion engine whose cylinders are arranged in a radial formation, like the spokes of a wheel. The radial engine was more reliable and easier to maintain than previous engines, and Lindbergh immediately saw its advantages.

It would weigh less and would allow a plane to go much farther than a conventional engine would. If this engine were placed in the right kind of plane—one that was lightweight and could carry lots of fuel—it might allow him to cross the ocean. Funded by some businessmen he knew in St. Louis, Lindbergh found a manufacturer who would build the plane to his specifications at the Ryan Company of San Diego, California.

Workers there found that Lindbergh's design was unusual. His plane had few instruments because he felt too many would add unnecessary weight to the machine. Some people thought the plane was improperly equipped for such a daring flight. Lindbergh's stripped-down airplane was essentially a flying gas tank, they said. They were right. But that did not bother Lindbergh. A plane that could carry more fuel than any other plane would give him the edge he needed. He decided to name the plane *The Spirit of St. Louis,* in appreciation of the support he received from his friends there.

When the Ryan Company finished building the plane, Lindbergh flew it from San Diego to St. Louis in fourteen

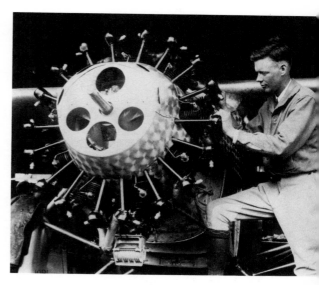

Charles Lindbergh examines his revolutionary air-cooled engine. This efficient engine weighed less than conventional water-cooled engines, making longer flights possible.

hours, a new record. After stopping briefly, he flew on to New York, going from coast to coast in twenty-one hours. That in itself was an incredible feat in 1926, earning Lindbergh coverage in newspapers and on the radio across the country. He had not even started his flight across the ocean and already he was a national hero. People everywhere began anticipating his daring attempt.

With Fingers Crossed, the World Watches

In the days before Lindbergh took off, everyone had an opinion about him and what his chances were. Many experienced flyers felt that Lindbergh was not only a daring young man but also an absolute fool. He planned to fly across the Atlantic alone, without even a radio or a life raft. Others who were going to attempt the flight carried emergency provisions, and some even

Charles Lindbergh stands by his plane, The Spirit of St. Louis. *He became a hero overnight after his solo, nonstop flight over the Atlantic on May 20, 1927.*

flew three-engine planes so that if one failed, they would still have two more engines. But most important, none of them planned to fly alone. It would be a long, tiring journey, and the pilot would need to rest at some point.

Lindbergh was well aware of the precautions being taken by other pilots. But he knew exactly what he was doing. He chose to fly without another person, an extra engine, or emergency equipment because they would all weigh down his aircraft. He had calculated the advantages and disadvantages of carrying each of these things. He rejected them all. He believed that to go the distance, he would have to travel as light as possible. Leaving everything nonessential behind and carrying more gasoline would allow him to make it all the way across the ocean. While the public debated the merits of Lindbergh's risky strategy, others who planned to make the flight were not faring well. The danger involved in the journey was very real, as a series of tragic accidents demonstrated. Pilot Rene Fonck, taking off on a practice flight, crashed and burned his plane, the *America,* in September 1926. He survived, but two of his four-man crew did not. Another Lindbergh rival, Noel Davis, and his copilot, died in a crash in what was supposed to be their last flight before leaving for Paris. Finally, less than two weeks before Lindbergh made his flight, Charles Nungesser and Francis Coli left Paris in the *White Bird* and flew west across the Atlantic. When Lindbergh left New York twelve days later, they still had not been heard from. They never were.

Despite the growing sense of peril, Lindbergh was eager to make his journey. After waiting days for the weather to improve, he took off from Roosevelt Field on Long Island, New York, on May 20, 1927, into a dense fog. His perceived lack of caution had generated much debate. But once he left, there was no more discussion of Lindbergh's foolhardiness. Regardless of whether they agreed with his daring approach, people across the nation and around the world hoped for the best as he took off on his heroic voyage. On the evening of May 20, 1927, many people dropped whatever they were doing as their thoughts drifted up into the dark night sky over the ocean. Families stayed up to listen anxiously to hourly reports on the radio. The suspense only mounted, since no one had any reliable information as to where Lindbergh was and how he was doing. They could only wonder and hope.

The pilot himself did little wondering. It was cold in *The Spirit of St. Louis,* and a sheet of ice covered the plane. He heard thunder in the distance. He was not one to wonder about what effect his flight might have on the world anyway. Instead, he concentrated fully on the job of flying. He was so focused the he forgot about the sandwiches he had stowed behind the seat before he left. He dozed off once, only to be awakened as the plane fell into a tailspin. He pulled it back up and stayed awake the rest of the way.

"Lucky Lindy" Takes Paris by Storm

When the long night turned into morning, Lindbergh was above the coast of France. He turned his airplane toward Paris with no idea of what was in store for him. *The Spirit of St. Louis* was instantly mobbed when he arrived in Paris, 33 1/2 hours after he had departed from New York. The crowd swarmed past police and toward *The Spirit of St. Louis* so quickly that Lindbergh was afraid the still-whirling propeller might cut someone. As soon as the propeller stopped and he stepped out of the plane, the mob was upon him, grabbing for souvenirs. In the confusion, a man grabbed Lindbergh's flight helmet and goggles. The crowd assumed the man was Lindbergh and carried him away, while the real Lindbergh made his escape.

In the weeks and months that followed, "Lucky Lindy" received medals and trophies everywhere he went. He spoke to the French Assembly and the British Parliament. When he returned to the United States, on board a Navy ship that had been sent especially for him, an entire flotilla of warships fired their guns in a salute. He dined with

Charles Lindbergh's famous New York-to-Paris flight received extensive media coverage and international acclaim.

President and Mrs. Coolidge, addressed a joint session of Congress, then received the Distinguished Flying Cross in a ceremony on the Washington Mall. Next, he went to New York, where an estimated four million people—equal to the population of the city—turned out for the biggest ticker tape parade the city had ever seen.

Lindbergh was not the first to cross the Atlantic in an airplane. In fact, he was the seventy-ninth. But he was the first to do it alone, which impressed people deeply. He had relied on his own intelligence to design the plane and on his own courage and endurance to make a risky flight into the unknown. Going solo, he had reconfirmed that amazing things were possible with airplanes. He collected the twenty-five thousand dollar prize, but the fame thrust upon him was totally unexpected and perhaps unwanted. Yet his status as an international hero opened many doors—for Lindbergh and for the growing field of aviation.

A Spokesperson for the Air-Minded

After his success, Lindbergh was in great demand as a speaker, and he willingly spread the word about the wonderful potential of airplanes. Financed by the Guggenheim Fund for the Promotion of Aeronautics, he embarked on a tour of the United States in *The Spirit of St. Louis*. He stopped in eighty-two cities and towns and did much to promote the coming era of aerial mass transport. He was also an excellent goodwill ambassador for the United States. In 1928, he flew *The Spirit of St. Louis* on a tour of Central and South America. He won over crowds at every stop and generated good feelings toward the United States.

In Mexico, Lindbergh met Anne Morrow, daughter of the U.S. ambassador to that country. They fell in love and were married in 1929. He taught her to fly, and together they flew to China via the Arctic Circle. Two years later, they flew along the Atlantic coasts of Europe, Africa, and South America. She wrote about the trips in two books, *North to the Orient* and *Listen, the Wind!* Both were best-sellers. Like other women pilots, Anne Morrow Lindbergh helped convince the public that flying was a safe activity. For many people, their only experience with airplanes was witnessing the daring stunts of barnstormers. They assumed that all flying was perilous. Women pilots

In 1928, Amelia Earhart was the first transatlantic woman passenger. In 1937, she and navigator Frederick Noonan disappeared on an attempted flight around the world.

showed that a person did not have to be a crazed "birdman" to fly a plane.

Another famous woman pilot was Amelia Earhart. In 1928 she became the first woman to fly across the Atlantic, as a passenger in a plane designed by Anthony Fokker. He was the same man who had designed for the Germans a plane with a machine-gun that was synchronized with the propellers. In 1932, Earhart flew solo from Newfoundland to Ireland in about fifteen hours. Later that year, she became the first woman to fly solo across the United States. In 1935, she also became the first person to fly alone from Hawaii to California. In 1937, she and navigator Frederick J. Noonan set out to fly around the world. They mysteriously disappeared between New Guinea and Howland Island.

Other early flight pioneers included Wiley Post and navigator Harold Gatty. They departed from Long Island in June 1931 in a Lockheed Vega named *Winnie Mae*. The Vega had a Wright Whirlwind engine, and a cigar-shaped, plywood fuselage. It also had a one-piece wing, without the bracing struts that other planes had required for stability. Post and Gatty departed in the *Winnie Mae* for a successful nine-day flight around the world. Post went around the world again in 1933.

The Airplane Business Booms

The publicity generated by these dramatic flights helped build support for flight in general. Such adventures also showed people that money could be made flying. If so many people be-

Wiley Post stands in front of the Winnie Mae. *In 1931, Post and navigator Harold Gatty took the plane on a nine-day flight around the world.*

came so excited when someone flew around the world, then clearly some of them would be interested in flying to faraway places themselves.

Various airplane-related enterprises were soon in motion. With airplanes getting bigger and more powerful, transporting goods by air became an alternative to trucking or sending things by train. Travelers began to realize that they could get somewhere much faster through the air, and the tourism industry began to grow. Passenger airlines formed in the mid 1930s to take advantage of the new travel market. It became important to make even bigger, better, and faster airplanes. To help the aeronautics industry meet the demand for new airplanes, many universities began degree programs in aeronautical engineering. Factories had to be set up to build the new airplanes, and new airports had to be constructed. Airplanes became an important part of the national economy. Airplanes were making an impact on people's lives in many ways.

People who operated businesses learned that they could keep smaller inventories on hand, since supplies could rapidly be flown in when the need arose. In publishing, the delivery of newspapers and magazines by airplane made it possible for publications to be delivered to a wider geographic area. In manufacturing, company managers were able to visit plants and sites around the country. This resulted in improved communications and better performance within the company.

Temporary operations made use of airplanes, too. During Prohibition, planes were used by illegal bootleggers to transport alcoholic beverages as well as by the government agents who tried to catch the bootleggers. Manufacturers of small planes found that some potential buyers were most interested in how many bottles the airplane could hold.

Spotting Fish, Fires, and Urban Growth Patterns

More legitimate uses for airplanes were found by government agencies. The Bureau of Fisheries discovered during the 1920s that schools of fish could be easily spotted from an airplane. The location of the fish would be reported to fishing ships, saving them many fruitless days of wandering the ocean trying to locate fish. Also in the 1920s, the Forest Service found that planes were useful in spotting forest fires. This was especially true after electrical storms, when many small fires were started by lightning. Besides making it easier to monitor millions of acres of forest, airplanes were also used to quickly dispatch fire fighters and supplies to the scene of the fire. Later, special airplanes were developed to drop water and fire-fighting chemicals on fires.

Another benefit of airplane development was the advancement of meteorology. The U.S. Weather Bureau greatly expanded its forecasting activities in order to provide pilots with better weather information. People across the nation benefited from more accurate and regular forecasts.

Aerial surveying also became an important activity. Photographs taken from above urban areas gave city planners a new perspective on the growth of cities. These pictures gave them a much better idea than the charts and graphs they had relied upon before of what was taking place on the ground.

The use of airplanes for such specialized purposes revealed their exciting potential. With different designs, planes could be built for many different uses. Airplanes could be small, fast, and maneuverable, or they could be large, powerful, and capable of hauling heavy payloads. The performance of a specific plane was just a matter of building it to the correct specifications. It had become clear that any job that required moving people or things from place to place could probably be done with an airplane better and faster than it had been done before.

The Business of Building Better Planes

Designing and building airplanes was not a job that any one person could do alone. As the Wrights had learned building their first airplane, success depended on collaboration. The Wrights had combined their thinking skills and engineering knowledge to unlock the secrets of powered flight. They had also

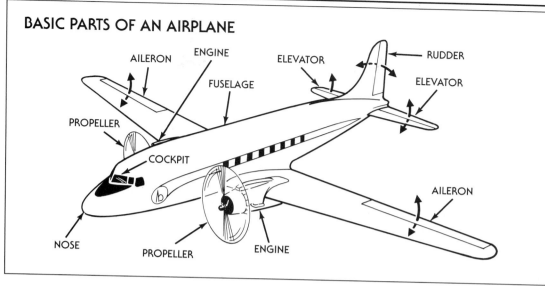

BASIC PARTS OF AN AIRPLANE

AILERON
ENGINE
ELEVATOR
RUDDER
FUSELAGE
ELEVATOR
PROPELLER
COCKPIT
AILERON
NOSE
PROPELLER
ENGINE

relied upon the expert workmanship of mechanic Charlie Taylor to help them put together the pieces of their flying machine.

After those first flyers of the Wrights, planes soon became bigger, more powerful, and more sophisticated. Putting together the various parts into a machine that flew as it should became a complex job that required planning, coordination, and the teamwork of experts. Specialists were required in engine design and in aerodynamics, for example. Together, many people had to decide the best way to build a safe and efficient plane.

It was also a very competitive business. Whenever one manufacturer made an improvement in design, others tried to duplicate it and, if possible,

U.S. aviator and airplane manufacturer Glenn Curtiss used aluminum and steel in the development of stronger, more sophisticated airplanes.

A worker constructs an airplane part in a Wright factory. Aviators and engineers continually updated aeronautical designs in their quest for improved aircraft.

THE PISTON-PROPELLER ENGINE

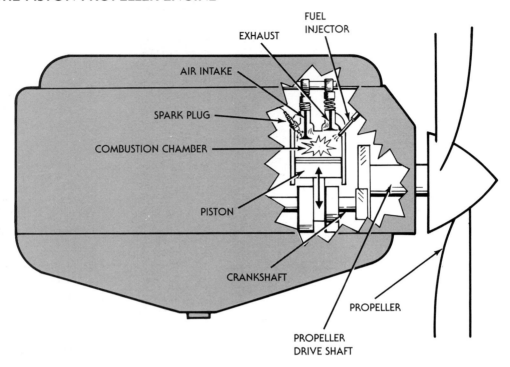

FUEL INJECTOR

EXHAUST

AIR INTAKE

SPARK PLUG

COMBUSTION CHAMBER

PISTON

CRANKSHAFT

PROPELLER

PROPELLER DRIVE SHAFT

The piston-propeller engine was the first source of thrust powerful and economical enough to permit the construction of large airplanes. Most engines of this type contained three or more cylinders which operate like the cylinder shown above. First, air and fuel mix in the cylinder's combustion chamber, where they are ignited by a spark. The ensuing combustion drives a piston, which is connected to a crankshaft. As the pistons move up and down, they turn the crankshaft, which turns the propeller.

on it even further. In this way, the best features of new airplane designs quickly became industry standards.

Companies started by Orville Wright and Glenn Curtiss were two of the earliest airplane manufacturers. Throughout the 1920s, the Wright Company, the Curtiss Aeroplane and Motor Corporation, and other companies made slow but steady progress. They discovered better materials and developed better designs. They found that combinations of aluminum and steel were stronger than the wood, wire, and canvas that the first planes were made of. These metals became useful in other industries too. They were used to make household appliances, automobiles, and other goods. The auto industry also benefited from research in aerodynamics, when it later became important to design fuel-efficient cars. Sleek cars mimicked the streamlined airplane shape that reduced wind resis-

With the advent of the first passenger planes in the 1930s, people had access to faster and more comfortable travel.

tance and allowed the vehicle to travel using less energy.

These advances were incidental to the real aim of the air-minded, however. Most of all, they wanted to allow more people to fly. An initial success came in the 1930s, when the first passenger planes appeared. In England, the Handley Pages H.P. 42 and H.P. 45 made regular flights from London to Cairo, Egypt, and Cape Town, South Africa. Flights also went from London to Paris.

These first H.P. planes were large and luxurious, and they featured hot meals in flight. They cruised at about one hundred miles per hour, but their piston-powered propellers were loud and caused considerable vibration during flight. This was an unavoidable problem with the internal-combustion engine. These early passenger planes offered people faster, more comfortable travel. But they only hinted at the speed and convenience that would soon be available.

A major improvement over these early planes was the Douglas DC-3, introduced in the United States in 1933. More rugged than previous passenger planes, its sturdy construction allowed it to carry up to nine thousand pounds, or about twenty-one passengers. With twin propellers and a long, wide wing,

the DC-3 was designed to be durable and easy to fly. It has been estimated that by 1938, DC-3s carried 95 percent of all airline traffic in the United States. They were also being used by thirty foreign airlines. About fourteen thousand were built, and many were still in service more than fifty years later.

The Persistent Dream of the Personal Plane

The progress in passenger planes was exciting. But many people still believed that they would one day have their own personal airplanes. It was an old dream—flight for all. Henry Ford had made his Model T available to practically everyone by mass-producing the reliable car on an assembly line. Some thought it was only a matter of time before he or someone else did the same thing with airplanes. Ford did, in fact, start manufacturing airplanes in 1925, building an eight-passenger aircraft. The next year, he came out with a twelve-passenger tri-motor airplane.

But what the public really wanted was the Model T of airplanes. So in 1926, Ford announced a prototype of an inexpensive airplane designed to be available to anyone. The small, single-

The Waterman Arrowbile, designed to be both an airplane and a car, never caught public interest. It was impractical and did not perform well.

seat machine created tremendous enthusiasm among the public. But two years later, Henry Brooks, a pilot and friend of Ford's, was killed in a crash while piloting one of the Ford planes. Saddened by the death of his friend, Ford suspended production and five years later stopped making planes altogether.

Still, the idea of an airplane in every garage persisted. In 1933, during Franklin Delano Roosevelt's first administration, Eugene Vidal, director of the Bureau of Air Commerce, announced that the government would spend $500,000 to develop a "poor-man's airplane." It would sell for about $700, which was about $300 less than any airplane then on the market. Made of metal, it would have two or three seats, and it would be so easy to fly that anyone could learn.

Airplane developers thought the plan was ridiculous. A plane simply could not be built that cheaply, no matter how small. Also, piloting was an acquired skill. To make an easy-to-fly plane would require programming some of the complicated functions so that they were automatic. But if, for instance, there were only one programmed way for a plane to make a turn, the pilot would lose much of the control of the plane. In flight it is im-

portant to be able to react precisely to the circumstances. If the pilot had less control because the plane had been programmed to fly a certain way, it could be a dangerous ride.

These concerns did not stop Vidal. He eventually awarded contracts to five developers for prototypes of the poor man's airplane. These yielded some interesting ideas. But none of them ever made it into production. Probably the most fascinating little airplane was the Waterman Arrowbile. Designed to be "roadable," it was capable of being driven on the highway as well as flown through the air. Powered by propellers in back, it was an oversize tricycle, with a clutch and transmission, headlights, little fenders, and license plates. But by trying to be both a plane and a car, it was not acceptable as either. It was slow and unresponsive as an airplane and too small and uncomfortable to be practical as a car. The Arrowbile was a good try that never caught on.

Ever since the Wrights' accomplishments became public knowledge, people had hoped that the airplane would succeed as a personal vehicle that would give every person greater freedom. It never lived up to that expectation. The Wrights' invention, however, exceeded all hopes in another arena.

Airplanes in World War II

Although the airplane did not have a decisive impact on the outcome of World War I, its use had shown that battles would never be fought the same way again. Twenty years later, airplane development had steadily evolved and advanced tremendously. Many small changes had occurred. Before, wings were braced by wires to the fuselage of the plane, for instance. Now those wires were hidden inside the wing, giving the plane a cleaner aerodynamic shape. Multiengine planes became the rule, rather than the exception. Military leaders in 1939 realized that the airplane could make troop and supply movements more convenient. It had the potential to be the most versatile and powerful weapon ever. Air power became a critical factor in how World War II started and how it was fought.

German dive bombers soar in flight. Germany's powerful air force, called the Luftwaffe, *spurred other nations to develop better airplanes.*

The Unfriendly Skies

During World War II, German bombers take off for an attack on Belgrade, Yugoslavia.

In violation of the Treaty of Versailles, established at the end of World War I, Germany secretly developed a powerful air force and in September 1939 used it to attack Poland. In response, Great Britain and France declared war on Germany, and World War II was under way. Airplanes were key to the Germans' success. Their strategy was to take control of the skies with their air force, called the *Luftwaffe,* so that their tanks and troops could move on the

ground unchallenged. The *Luftwaffe's* large bombers were sent out with escorts of small fighter planes to defend them against any attack.

While Poland and France quickly fell, Britain developed an air force of its own and succeeded in holding off the Germans, despite daily bombings of British cities. On December 7, 1941, Japan and the United States entered the war. Japan's surprise Sunday morning attack on Pearl Harbor, Hawaii, was achieved with small fighter planes, dive bombers, and torpedo bombers. Using their air power to its full potential, the Japanese first sank much of the U.S. Navy's Pacific fleet, then sank much of the British Pacific fleet, too.

Better airplanes were a necessity, and the United States, Germany, and Japan all geared up to produce new warplanes. Warplanes fit into two categories, bombers or fighters. The name of a plane often included the letter B or F, indicating which type it was. Both types of planes had improved since the last war. More powerful engines gave these airplanes the ability to go faster and farther. The better long-range capability of bombers and the fighters' ability to strike more quickly than ever gave armies more targets to hit. These factors totally changed the strategy of war. Instead of millions of men dying in the trenches as in World War I, now there were mass bombings. This was a new concept, and it became known as total war.

In total war, enemy troops and military facilities were targets, but so were civilian facilities like airplane factories, ports, bridges, dams, and even cathedrals. The result was devastation on a huge scale. London was one of the most heavily bombed cities. The German cities of Cologne, Dusseldorf, and Dresden were turned into raging fire storms by explosives dropped from bombers.

Airplanes also changed the way wars were fought at sea. In the Battle of the Coral Sea for instance, no ship on

Aircraft carriers housed and launched dozens of fighter planes during World War II. This system enabled the military to coordinate their attacks at sea.

either side saw an enemy ship. The fighting was all plane-to-plane or between planes and ships. The Americans depended heavily on the Gruman F4F Wildcat, a rugged fighter plane built for air-to-air combat. The Wildcat was coated with a tough armor that resisted bullets, and it had a rubber-lined gas tank that would seal itself if punctured by a bullet. It was armed with six Browning fifty-millimeter machine guns. Eight thousand Wildcats were built, and they served mostly in the South Pacific during the first half of the war.

Big Bombers and "Little Friends"

Wildcats and other fighters were launched from aircraft carriers, also a new development. Improved navigation through use of radio communications allowed the organization of large-scale operations from ships. Dozens of airplanes from several carriers could be coordinated in a single attack. In the Battle of Midway, the turning point of the war in the Pacific, fifty-four Douglas Dauntless SBD dive bombers launched from the carriers *Enterprise* and *Yorktown* helped the Allies to defeat the

Planes such as these B-17s were mass-produced in airplane factories for World War II.

Japanese fleet. The Dauntless was a metal, single-winged plane fitted with a powerful radial engine. It carried one-thousand-pound bombs. Dauntless pilots would cruise at seventeen thousand feet, then dive to twenty-five hundred feet and release their bombs on Japanese warships.

Another bomber that helped win the war was the Boeing B-17 Flying Fortress. Used extensively in Europe after the Allied invasion of June 6, 1944, the B-17 was a large, sturdy plane. It had a one-hundred-foot wingspan and four engines. It weighed more than thirty tons. The B-17 Flying Fortress carried a crew of nine. The bombardier sat in the Plexiglas nose of the plane, where he operated a machine-gun and the switches to open the bay doors that would release the bombs. Behind and above him sat the navigator and two pilots. Above them, an engineer worked the gun turret on top of the plane, and a radioman sat in the back. There were

Fighter planes such as this one were launched from aircraft carriers. They did not have to go far to release their bombs on enemy warships.

German air force bombers fly in groups to protect themselves from enemy aircraft.

also two waist gunners who sat in the turret in the bottom of the plane behind the bay doors, and a tail gunner.

Gunners on the B-17 tried to fend off attackers as the plane approached its target, often German oil refineries and airplane factories. The B-17 did its job well but was vulnerable to attack by

Japanese kamikaze pilots deliberately crash bomb-bearing planes into Allied ships. The Japanese considered these suicide missions the ultimate act of patriotism.

quick and numerous German fighter planes, especially when they attacked from straight in front. One-third of the 12,731 Flying Fortresses built were shot down. Many more would have been lost if it were not for the development of the North American P-51 Mustang.

The Mustang was a small, fast, and acrobatic plane. It was a powerful, single-seat fighter with the longer range of a bomber. Equipped with a Rolls-Royce engine, it could go 430 miles per hour at twenty-two thousand feet and was well-armed with six machine-guns. Sixteen thousand Mustangs were built and just in time. The plane came out in the autumn of 1944, when many B-17s were being shot down by the *Luftwaffe* and Allied air power was faltering. Nearly helpless against quick German fighters, B-17 crew members began referring to the Mustangs as "little friends," and with good reason.

With its superior quickness, the P-51 was adept at shooting down German fighters. Staying close to the big bombers, a squadron of P-51s could chase off German attackers and allow the B-17 to fly unmolested to its target area. In huge air battles with as many as eight hundred Mustangs escorting up

The Boeing Flying Fortress was large and powerful, yet vulnerable to quick German fighter planes, which attacked the Boeings head on.

to thirteen hundred B-17s, the bombing of Germany resumed, and Berlin was reduced to rubble. In desperation, the Germans worked day and night to develop jet bombers and missiles, but they were not in time. On May 7, 1945, Germany surrendered.

The war continued in the Pacific, where at least half of the U.S. ships lost in the Pacific were sunk by Japanese kamikazes. Kamikazes were suicidal pilots who purposely flew their aircraft directly at U.S. ships, effectively turning their airplanes into large, guided bombs.

An Airplane Delivers a Deadly New Weapon

Another Boeing bomber, the B-29 Superfortress, was twice as powerful and much heavier than the B-17. It also had remote-control machine-guns. The Superfortress delivered the final blow of the war. An atomic bomb was dropped from the B-29 Superfortress *Enola Gay* onto Hiroshima, Japan, on August 6, 1945. Another B-29, *Bockscar* dropped an atomic bomb on Nagasaki on August 9, 1945. Japan surrendered on August 15, 1945, and World War II ended.

From start to finish, the use of airplanes was a major strategic factor in the war. The wholesale destruction they made possible caused some people to question the real value of airplanes, which had once been seen as a potentially great instrument of peace. In 1943, Senator Bennett C. Clark of Missouri said that the invention of the airplane was the "greatest disaster that has ever happened to mankind."

Orville Wright felt differently:

I don't have any regrets about my part in the invention of the airplane, though no one could deplore more than I do the destruction it has caused. I feel about the airplane much as I do in regard to fire. That is I regret all the terrible damage caused by fire. But I think it is good for the human race that someone discovered how to invent fires and that it is possible to put fire to thousands of important uses.

The Jet Age

Following World War II, it was nearly impossible *not* to become air-minded. Airplanes seemed to be everywhere. Millions of people had flown in them as part of their duties in the armed services. Many others worked in factories building airplanes. Even those who did not encounter them directly saw airplanes often on movie newsreels. At home, building detailed model airplanes became a popular hobby. The airplane simply could not be ignored. It had become a fact of everyday life.

Just as World War I had been the great accelerator of airplane development, World War II also resulted in improved airplane designs. Support systems of runways and fuel availability greatly expanded. Navigation had also improved. Radio signals beamed out from landing fields let pilots know if they were on course. Instruments like the gyroscope, which shows what direction a plane is flying, and the altimeter, which measures altitude, gave pilots more information about their plane's performance. In addition, World War II produced many thousands of trained pilots who became available for jobs in civil aviation.

Also, the war fundamentally changed the way people thought about travel. Before the war, a trip from the United States to Europe or Africa required a two-week voyage on an ocean liner and then two more weeks traveling back. After the war, people knew that faraway places could be reached in hours, rather than days or weeks.

The biggest change in aviation to come out of World War II was the development of the jet engine, although it came too late to be a major factor in the war. In the late 1920s, Frank Whittle, a pilot and flight instructor in Great Britain's Royal Air Force, had written a thesis on alternate ways of propelling aircraft. He came up with the idea of equipping an airplane with a gas turbine, which was an old idea. But Whittle's jet engine would update the old gas turbine and greatly improve airplane performance.

A New Spin on an Old Idea

The principle behind Whittle's jet engine is simple. It is a variation of the gas-turbine engine, patented in 1791 by John Barber. Drawings made by Barber show the essential features of the gas-turbine engine: a compressor, which pulls in air and passes it to a continuous-flow combustion chamber, where the air is mixed with fuel and ignited; and a turbine, which is a rotary engine that spins as a result of the hot gases (the exhaust) being expelled from the combustion chamber. The energy generated by the spinning turbine may be used for thrust, or to spin a propeller. This kind of engine is known as a turboprop.

HOW A JET ENGINE WORKS

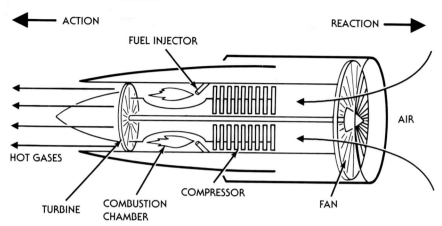

A jet engine works on the principle of jet propulsion, which states that for every action there is an equal and opposite reaction. With a jet engine, it works like this:

A large fan draws air into the air compressors. The air compressor compress the air, or raise its pressure. Then the pressurized air flows into the combustion chambers, where it is heated by burning kerosene or paraffin. Next, the hot, high-pressure air rushes toward the exhaust. On the way, it passes through turbines, which drive the compressors and the fan. Finally, the hot, high-pressure air leaves the jet with great force. This action causes an equal and opposite reaction, which drives the jet forward.

Working from this simple model, Whittle and others after him designed more sophisticated jet turbines. They used strong, lightweight new alloys to make combustion chambers that could withstand the heat and stress of burning jet fuel. Scientists found that jet engines could produce far greater thrust than was possible with propellers. For instance, the Wrights' first engine generated twelve horsepower. The engine in a DC-7 today generates thirty-four hundred horsepower at takeoff.

Whittle had tried to convince the British Air Ministry in 1929 that his innovative engine might benefit the Royal Air Force, if the British government would invest the money required. But the government was not persuaded, and Whittle's idea was turned down. He had his design patented anyway in January 1930. After working as a flight instructor for several years, he finally found private investors who were willing to take a chance on his idea in 1936. With their funding, he established a company called Power Jets Limited.

Meanwhile, scientists in Nazi Germany were also working on a jet engine. In 1939, Ernst Heinkel's aircraft company produced the Heinkel He-178, the first successful gas-turbine plane. Then, near the end of the war, Allied pilots reported seeing an amazing new German fighter plane. It was

Frank Whittle stands by his revolutionary jet propulsion unit. This system had a major impact on airplane design and performance.

the Messerschmitt Me-262. It did not have a propeller, and it flew faster than anything they had ever seen. These sightings may have been what convinced the British government that Whittle's design was worth investigating after all.

In 1941 the British had a jet airplane ready for test flight. The Gloster E28/39 flew successfully. The jet design was soon exported to the United States, where the General Electric company began producing experimental planes for the war effort, using the Whittle engine. The first of these American jets, the Bell XP-59 Airacomet, flew in October 1942. By 1944, the British-made Gloster Meteor was in full production and was used by the Royal Air Force near the end of the war. But both the Meteor and the Messerschmitt Me-262 were developed

The British-made Gloster Meteor, equipped with a jet engine, was used by the Royal Air Force at the end of World War II.

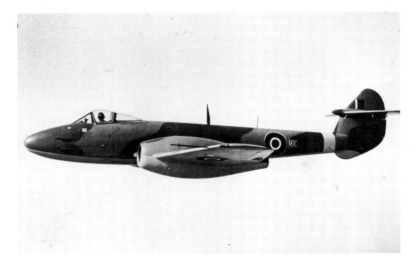

too late in the war to have an impact on its outcome.

The jet engine had many advantages over the piston-driven engines that preceded it. Instead of becoming less efficient at high speeds and high altitudes as the piston engine did, the jet engine became *more* efficient under those conditions. It allowed aircraft to go much faster and higher with less vibration than the conventional piston-driven craft. Propeller-driven airplanes could fly at a maximum of about 450 miles per hour. Jets, properly designed, would be able to go much faster. For these reasons, the jet was an exciting advance for military aviation designers. They eagerly began developing new jet planes.

On September 17, 1947, President Harry Truman signed legislation creating the U.S. Air Force. This incited a boom in the development of jets for the military.

Another Boom in Aviation

The timing was perfect for another boom in the aviation business. When the war ended, there were still many airplane factories that had been set up for rapid production of warplanes. With this manufacturing structure in place and the reality of jet power emerging, military aviation was ready to progress. Recognizing that airplanes would be a major factor in national defense from then on, President Harry S. Truman signed legislation on September 17, 1947. This legislation created the U.S. Air Force out of the old U.S. Army Air Service. With this separate

U.S. jet pilots stand in front of the first U.S. jet fighter, the Lockheed F-80 Shooting Star. This jet was able to reach a speed of up to 580 miles per hour.

This powerful Lockheed F-80 Shooting Star has a 39-foot wing span, a length of over 34 feet, and a weight of 15,000 pounds.

branch of the military dedicated to aviation, the research and development of jet planes became a priority.

Several jets were quickly produced using the standard straight-wing airplane design. But some forward-thinking designers had a new idea. Perhaps a more aerodynamic wing shape would take better advantage of the increased power offered by jets. These designers proposed that the wings and tail section be swept back at a thirty-five-degree angle rather than the standard ninety degrees. Data captured from a World War II German aerodynamics research center confirmed what American designers suspected: wind tunnel tests performed by the Germans showed that the swept-wing design would allow a jet to fly faster and more efficiently. Captured Messerschmitt jets were also studied.

The first operational U.S. jet fighter was the Lockheed F-80 Shooting Star, introduced in 1945. With a thirty-nine-foot wingspan, the fighter jet could reach a speed of 580 miles per hour at twenty-five thousand feet. A few years later, the North American XP-86 was developed using the swept-wing design. Other innovations and improvements emerged as manufacturers continued to experiment with new designs and materials. In performance tests, these new jet planes broke all the old records set by piston-powered aircraft.

Just as in the early days of flight, courageous pilots were eager to set new flight records of speed and distance. Flight testing soon became a science, as engineers worked to develop a jet plane that could withstand the pressure of flying faster than the speed of sound.

Pushing the Limits of Possibility

Named for Austrian physicist and ballistics expert Ernst Mach, a Mach number is the ratio between the speed of an object and the speed of sound. A plane traveling at Mach 3.0 would be traveling at three times the speed of sound. In theory, traveling this fast was possible, but no one had ever done it. To reach supersonic speeds—speeds

Ernst Mach of Austria developed the Mach number, in which speed of an airplane is expressed as a multiple of the speed of sound.

equal to or up to five times greater than the speed of sound—would be to venture into the realm of the unknown.

In their quest for greater speed, scientists turned to rocket technology as a possible solution. As in jet propulsion, rockets, first created by the Chinese in about A.D. 1100, burn fuel within a chamber to create thrust. But while jets use an intake valve to mix air with fuel, rockets burn a mixture of more powerful propellants within a closed chamber to generate even greater thrust.

Liquefied gases, such as hydrogen and oxygen, create a powerful reaction when burned. Scientists found that when these types of gases are mixed with solids like nitroglycerin and then ignited, the resulting thrust might be enough to reach Mach 1, or the speed of sound.

A plane could not carry enough fuel to generate more than two or three minutes of the thrust that would be needed to break the sound barrier.

That problem was solved by launching the first rocket-propelled aircraft, the bullet-shaped X-1, from another plane already in midair. On October 14, 1947, Chuck Yeager piloted the X-1 on its ninth flight, above the Mojave Desert in Southern California. Nicknamed "Glamorous Glennis" after Yeager's wife, the X-1 was dropped out of a B-29 Superfortress at thirty-five thousand feet. Yeager turned on the rockets and climbed to seventy thousand feet. A loud boom echoed through the desert as he became the first person to break the sound barrier. Yeager also set a new speed record of 670 miles per hour.

Enthralled with the idea of traveling faster than the speed of sound, the public followed Yeager's flight and those after it with great interest. Research on rocket-powered flight continued until development of the speedy X-15. First flown in 1959, it was fueled by a mix of liquid oxygen and ammonia. Pilot Joseph Walker achieved the world speed

On October 14, 1947, Chuck Yeager became the first person to break the sound barrier when he flew the X-1 over the Mojave Desert in Southern California.

On October 3, 1967, Joseph Walker achieved the world speed record of 4,520 miles per hour in the rocket-powered X-15.

View of the X-15, which exploded in flight, killing pilot Joseph Walker.

record of 4,520 miles per hour, or Mach 6.7, on October 3, 1967, in an X-15 that was launched in midair from a B-52.

Although rocket-powered aircraft could achieve incredible speeds, they did not seem very useful until later. In the early 1950s, jet-powered aircraft had more practical applications, especially for the military. Jet-engine technology played a crucial role in the military throughout the 1950s, as tensions mounted between the United States and the Soviet Union. Neither side wanted to be vulnerable to weapons like the atomic bombs that had been dropped on Japan at the end of World War II.

To bolster their national defenses, scientists in both countries worked to develop aircraft capable of flying faster, higher, and farther than ever before. They also developed sophisticated new weapons, such as heat-seeking missiles, which could track down an enemy jet

by the heat from its exhaust and then destroy it.

When one country made a breakthrough in technology, the other would scramble to catch up. Both sides depended on surveillance, espionage, and research to make sure their technology was up-to-date. U.S. and Soviet Union air power stayed evenly matched for years. Two military jets with comparable capabilities were the Soviet MiG-15 and the U.S. F-86 Sabre. Both jets were capable of climbing to about fifty thousand feet, and both had top speeds of about 680 miles per hour. During the Korean War, pilots flying these fighters often encountered each other over Korean airspace. Despite being evenly matched on paper, U.S. pilots won more often in the air. Credited with better training and more experience, U.S. pilots shot down 827 MiGs and lost only 78 Sabres.

The U.S. Air Force's fastest jet fighter, the North American F-86, attained speeds of up to 680 miles per hour.

The Streaking Comet

Jets had uses outside of the military, too. They were also being developed for civilian travel and transportation purposes. The first commercial transport jet, the British-made de Havilland Comet, was a fast, comfortable aircraft. Introduced in 1952, it was expensive to fly because it required so much fuel. Therefore, it was used for relatively short flights—from London to Rome and from Rome to Johannesburg. Several of the Comets tragically exploded in flight after just a few hours in service, however, and the remaining Comets were grounded. Following a thorough investigation, engineers found that the metal in some critical parts of the plane had weakened and cracked. These cracks would spread until the plane literally fell apart. De Havilland designers went back to the drawing board and later introduced the successful Comet IV.

In the United States, Boeing introduced several planes that would forever change the way that people travel. The Boeing 707 made its first flight in 1954. Travelers who had flown on noisy, relatively slow, propeller-driven planes soon became accustomed to the speed and comfort of traveling on the 707. It became the preferred way to travel. The 707 gained the prestige of providing presidential travel when one was ordered in 1959 to serve as Air Force One, the president's private jet. Another Boeing plane, the 704, was a big plane with four jet engines. It was the precursor of modern jets that many passengers fly in today.

Soon after the 704 was developed, the Douglas Aircraft Company, a Boeing competitor, introduced the DC-8, a longer jet that was capable of seating up to 250 people. Jets continued to grow ever larger until Boeing built the 747 "jumbo jet." It first flew in 1969 and could carry almost 500 passengers.

These large jetliners were purchased by airline companies that planned to provide long-distance passenger service to major cities around the country and

overseas. Regional airlines bought smaller propeller-driven planes like the DC-3, a surplus World War II plane, and carried passengers between smaller cities and from small towns to larger cities. The world became a network of destinations, none more than a day or so away from anywhere else. The term *jet set* was coined in 1951 to describe world travelers who took advantage of this fantastic mobility.

Commercial aircraft were also built for more specialized needs. Hoping to find a market among busy corporate executives, William Lear designed a six-seat jet capable of traveling at five hundred miles per hour at forty-five thousand feet. Lear used the sleek design of a jet fighter that had been scheduled to be produced by the government of Switzerland but was canceled. Transformed from a small jet fighter to a transport plane, the jet could barely hold six people and would not allow anyone to stand up straight. Despite these limitations, the Lear jet became a smashing success. It allowed elite business travelers to fly high above storms and turbulence and to zoom directly to their destinations, rather than wait for a scheduled airline flight. With its jet-fighter looks and superfast speed, the Lear jet became a symbol of corporate success.

The Controversial SST

For the average air traveler, however, the speed and convenience offered by the Lear jet was not available. Military jets had succeeded in breaking the sound barrier years before, but there were no commercial jets capable of traveling that fast. In the early 1960s,

(top) In the 1950s, the British developed the de Havilland Comet for civilian transportation. The comet became obsolete after several exploded in flight.
(middle) In 1954, the introduction of the Boeing 707 had a major impact on air travel. This model was popular for its comfort and speed.
(bottom) In 1969, crowds watch as the four-jet Douglas Aircraft DC-8 soars skyward. This was the largest jetliner to date.

The Lear Jet, named after creator William Lear, became a symbol of prestige. Its sleek design and speed made it especially popular among business travelers.

however, the United States, the Soviet Union, and a partnership between Britain and France all worked separately to develop a supersonic transport (SST) jet. Such an aircraft would take advantage of the many improvements that had occurred in every area of aviation, from aerodynamic and electronic innovations to more powerful engines. The SST would be capable of flying at Mach 2.7. It would transport travelers to different points around the world faster than ever.

As development on the SST progressed, manufacturers found that the high-powered jet was extremely loud and required great amounts of fuel. In the United States, the SST encountered opposition from environmental groups concerned about the effects of the incredible noise generated by the jet. Environmentalists were also concerned about the damage that its emissions might inflict on the ozone layer high up in the earth's atmosphere. (The ozone layer is a layer of gases that surrounds the earth. It protects the earth from the sun's ultraviolet rays.)

One solution to the noise problem was to schedule the SST to follow routes that went over the water, where there were no people. But the super-

The Concorde SST, the supersonic commercial passenger plane developed by France and Britain, was first flown in 1976.

sonic plane would still generate incredible noise at takeoff. The controversy grew, and in 1971, the U.S. House of Representatives voted to halt funding of the SST project. The Soviet Union went ahead with its SST, but it was put out of service in 1977, after less than one year of operation. Only sixteen Concorde SSTs were built by the joint British-French project. Some of them now operate on flights from Paris to New York and Washington, D.C. Although its passengers are transported with amazing speed, few people can afford to fly on the SST. Tickets are unusually expensive due to the high cost of the fuel it uses. The aerospace industry, the industry that builds aircraft, wanted to make air travel affordable to more people. It concentrated on building airliners that were more fuel-efficient than the SST was. In helping to provide affordable air travel to everyone, aerospace manufacturers became a major part of the American economy by the 1970s. In 1965, for instance, airplanes worth $1.2 billion were delivered to the airlines. By 1975, that figure had risen to $3.8 billion. Jobs in manufacturing, service, and research were created. Many thousands of people still work in the aviation industry. Ticket agents, aerospace engineers, construction workers who help build airports, pilots, flight attendants, and ground personnel all help keep the airlines in business.

Today's jetliners incorporate an array of high-tech safety features, including life-support systems like drop-down oxygen masks and seat cushions that double as life preservers. Another important safety device is the so-called "black box."

This durable, fireproof box contains a computerized recorder that records flight data and a cockpit voice recorder. The flight-data recorder monitors the cockpit's instruments and keeps track of air speed, engine settings, altitude, and other flight information. The voice recorder captures everything that is said between pilots and air-traffic controllers. When a crash happens, investigators immediately begin looking for the small black box. It is located in the tail section of the aircraft, which usually receives the least impact in a crash. If they find the black box, investigators have a better chance of understanding why the crash happened and perhaps how future crashes can be avoided.

As the use of commercial aircraft continues to grow, one of the most high-pressure jobs in the industry is that of air-traffic controller. Using radio equipment and radar screens to communicate with pilots, air-traffic controllers coordinate the use of runways and the overcrowded air space around the nation's busiest airports. Directing an increasing volume of traffic, air-traffic controllers help pilots avoid accidents and keep airports running smoothly.

Military Aviation Today

The Lear jet and the SST incorporated some of the technological advances made in military aviation. Military planes, however, continued to improve far beyond commercial aviation throughout the 1960s. For example, one military aircraft produced in this era, the Gruman F-14 Tomcat, flies at Mach 2, twice the speed of sound. The Tomcat also has good maneuverability at slow speeds. Its "swing wings" give the F-14 its

(right)
In 1974, General Dynamics built this lightweight F-16. The forward-sweep wings give this jet fighter great stability and flexibility.

(below)
A three-quarter rear view of the F-16 fighter jet.

great flexibility. At takeoff, the wings are in the ninety-degree position that gives aircraft the lift necessary to leave the ground. When the F-14 is in flight, the wings can be swept back to a thirty-five degree angle. This gives the aircraft the stability needed for flight at very high speeds.

Military aircraft eventually began flying at altitudes where the pull of gravity is not as strong as it is on earth. In the atmosphere of near-space, pilots had to be equipped with supertight flight suits that offset the effects of zero gravity on the body. These special suits are outfitted with air bladders that squeeze the pilot's body to keep blood flowing to the brain so that the pilot does not pass out.

Such sophisticated features were costly to build. In 1974, the F-16 was developed by General Dynamics as a lightweight, "economy" jet fighter. At $14 million each, however, they cost more than expected. The more heavily armed F-15 goes for $17 million. Emerging technologies continue to improve the abilities of aircraft. High-altitude spy planes such as the U-2 now cruise as high as seventy thousand feet. In the early 1980s, the Northrop Corporation used new technology to create the sleek B-2, also known as the Stealth bomber. The smooth contours of the B-2 are designed to make it harder for radar to detect it. Its surface is covered with tiles that absorb radar waves. These features make the B-2 difficult if not impossible for radar to spot. But scientists are already developing better radar that would offset these advantages.

The Ultralights

The dream of a flying machine in every garage has still not been realized. But

Designer Burt Rutan, left, and pilots Jeanna Yeager and Dick Rutan pose in front of the Voyager *aircraft. In 1987, the* Voyager *made an historic flight by going around the world without stopping for fuel.*

there has been a growing interest in civil aviation over the decades. Many people bought used surplus planes, especially the Fairchild PT-19, a training plane, after World War II. But small, private planes like Cessna, Beechcraft, and Piper became more and more expensive, and few people were able to afford their own planes. As small planes became more expensive to own, pilot license applications declined in the 1980s. There are still many uses for smaller planes, however, from crop dusting to business travel.

Some people with a yearning to fly but without the money to invest in their own planes have turned to ultralight flyers. Like the first flying machines, these small-engine planes are open-air, carry only the pilot, and are of simple design. They allow the pilot to experience the thrill of open-air flight—much like the Wright brothers' early flights.

Ultralights and planes of all kinds travel every year to the Experimental Aircraft Association's (EAA) annual fly-in at Oshkosh, Wisconsin. Easily the largest aviation event in the world, it draws about one million air-minded people for one week every August to see the fifteen thousand aircraft that fly in. There are minijets, balloons, old military planes, and experimental flyers.

In the 1970s, an EAA member and Oshkosh fly-in regular named Burt Rutan designed several planes out of fiberglass and epoxy. These were lightweight planes that could go very far on little fuel. For years, he experimented with and improved upon his homemade flyers. Then in December 1986, his brother Dick Rutan and pilot Jeanna Yeager flew Burt Rutan's *Voyager* on a twenty-six thousand mile, nine-day, nonstop flight around the globe, without refueling. Like Charles Lindbergh's flight almost sixty years before, this trek focused the attention of millions on an aerial feat of endurance. The flight earned Yeager and Rutan the Presidential Citizen's Medal from President Ronald Reagan.

Linking the World

Inspiring events like Lindbergh's solo flight and the record-breaking saga of the *Voyager* touch people deeply. Such extraordinary breakthroughs are celebrated as triumphs of the human spirit, and they also lead to changes in the way we live. Lindbergh's flight paved the way for airlines to start organizing in the 1930s. Today, airlines serve thousands of businesspeople, vacationers,

The Voyager, *followed by a chase plane, flies over Southern California during its historic 1987 flight.*

and other travelers every day. Scattered families are able to reunite from distant places for holidays, weddings, and other important occasions. Millions of pieces of business mail are shipped across the country overnight, thanks to air express services.

Whether we want to send something to another place or to go ourselves, doing it is much easier than it was a few decades ago. In the jet age, the number of miles between places has become far less important. Choices that in the past were confined by distance are now more realistic options. These options have multiplied the possibilities in our lives.

No matter where in the world a person is today, he or she can be thousands of miles from that point the next day. In fact, it is now possible to fly to any point in the world in thirty-six hours or less. As a result, people from different cultures have been able to learn much about each other. They have shared ideas and have incorporated techniques and philosophies they have learned from other cultures into their own cultures. The result is that

humanity has become more a world culture than it was in the past.

The airplane has helped make the world a smaller place in many ways. Alaska and Hawaii, the forty-ninth and fiftieth states, respectively, are both far from the rest of the nation. They did not join the United States until 1959, when the jet age was well under way. Alaska and Hawaii probably would not have become part of the United States if it were not for the convenience of airplane travel to and from the forty-eight other states.

Flying has affected people's lives in very personal ways, too. Soon after jet travel was introduced, those who traveled by jet often complained of exhaustion and mental fatigue in the days following a flight. Late in the 1950s, scientists came up with an aptly named explanation: jet lag. In traveling rapidly from one time zone to another, the body struggles to readjust its inner rhythm of sleeping, eating, and other activities. Scientists found that without proper rest, jet travel is capable of wreaking havoc with a body's well-established routine.

Another problem with air travel is the danger and risks associated with flying. That air travel can be dangerous has been brought home many times by the deaths of famous Americans in plane crashes. Popular humorist and social critic Will Rogers died in 1935 in a crash with pioneering pilot Wiley Post. Notre Dame football coach Knute Rockne died in a plane crash in 1931, and rock and roll star Buddy Holly perished in a crash in the 1950s. Most people realize that airplane travel is safe and that the odds of a crash occurring are low. Yet some people refuse to fly. TV football commentator John Madden, for one, always goes by bus, despite a rigorous travel schedule.

The Entertainment World Takes Flight

Despite the risks, and maybe because of them, the theme of flight has also become a part of American entertainment. As early as 1910 there was a hit song about flying, called "Come Josephine in My Flying Machine." By the 1960s, a popular song was a somber ballad about "Leaving On a Jet Plane."

Over the years there have been many movies about military aviation. A 1928 movie called *Wings,* starring Gary Cooper, won the Academy Award as best picture of the year. In 1945, *Thunderbolt* portrayed P-47 fighters during the World War II Allied offensive in Italy; in 1959, *Twelve O'Clock High,* starring Gregory Peck, depicted the commander of a B-17 squadron in England.

In the late 1970s, author Tom Wolfe wrote *The Right Stuff,* which was about test pilots and astronauts, and the best-selling book was made into a movie. *Top Gun,* a popular movie of the 1980s, was about Navy pilots in a high-powered flight training school.

Some of the Hollywood lore surrounding flight may have added an element of romance to the idea of flying. But the age-old dream of flight has always stirred deep feelings. For some people, once they could fly, there was nothing else they could want. As early mail pilot Dean Smith described his chosen profession: "It was so alive and rich a life that any other conceivable choice seemed dull, prosaic, and humdrum."

For Charles Lindbergh and many others, time above the clouds became time for wonder and reflection on the vast world and each person's place in it—or above it:

> I may be flying a complicated airplane, rushing through space, but this cabin is surrounded by simplicity and thoughts set free of time and space. . . . Here, in *The Spirit of St. Louis,* I live in a different frame of time and space . . . . How detached the intimate things around me seem from the great world down below. How strange is this combination of proximity and separation. That ground—seconds away—thousands of miles away. This air, stirring mildly around me. That air, rushing by with the speed of a tornado, an inch beyond. These minute details in my cockpit. The grandeur of the world outside. The nearness of death. The longness of life.

CHAPTER 7

Aircraft in the Space Age

If Wilbur and Orville Wright had lived to see the SST, they would have been astonished. They would have found the size, speed, and noise of the big jet plane overwhelming when compared to their original invention. Likewise, if we could see the flying machines of the future, we would be amazed. Tomorrow's aircraft will integrate today's emerging technologies and will be radically different from the airplanes we are familiar with.

We have seen how two world wars helped spur the evolution of airplanes in the past. Modern, advanced aircraft are descendants of a third great wave of aeronautical development. The event that triggered this third wave and marked humanity's entry into the space age, was the flight of *Sputnik 1,* the first satellite to orbit the earth. The Soviet Union launched the basketball-size satellite on October 4, 1957. In the United States, a near-panic took hold as scientists and policymakers realized that the Soviets were ahead in the race to put humans in space.

In education, there was a sudden emphasis on science and engineering. In the aeronautics industry, rocket research became more critical than jet technology. The dream of faster, farther, first-ever flights became a major national priority. On May 21, 1961, President John F. Kennedy gave the United States the goal "before this decade is out, of landing a man on the moon and returning him safely to the earth. No single space project of this period will be more impressive to

An aeronautical engineer examines the Sputnik-1, *the Soviet satellite that orbited the earth on October 4, 1957.*

HOW THE SPACE SHUTTLE GETS ITS POWER

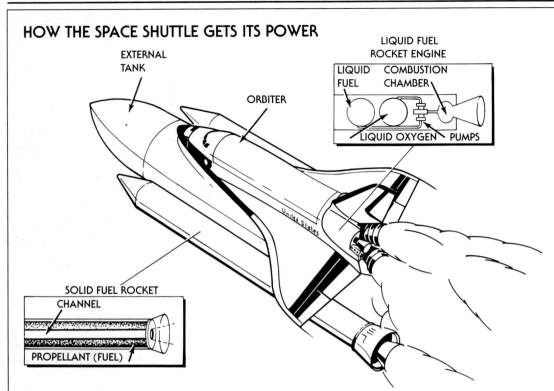

EXTERNAL TANK

ORBITER

LIQUID FUEL ROCKET ENGINE

LIQUID FUEL

COMBUSTION CHAMBER

LIQUID OXYGEN

PUMPS

SOLID FUEL ROCKET

CHANNEL

PROPELLANT (FUEL)

The space shuttle has five rocket engines to launch it into space. There are three liquid-fuel rocket engines located at the rear of the shuttle and two huge solid-fuel boosters fixed alongside it. The solid-fuel boosters burn up all their fuel within two minutes after the shuttle is launched. Then they detach from the shuttle and fall back to the earth.

The single largest structure in the shuttle configuration is the external fuel tank. This enormous, cone-shaped cylinder contains the liquid hydrogen and oxygen needed to fuel the shuttle's main engines. They use all the fuel in the external tank to get the shuttle moving fast enough to escape the pull of the earth's gravity. Then the huge tank detaches from the orbiter and falls to the earth. After this, the shuttle relies on its smaller liquid-fuel engines to maneuver into and out of orbit.

A solid-fuel rocket engine is like a

giant Roman candle. Inside its metal casing, the rocket is filled with solid, highly combustible fuel. The fuel surrounds an empty channel that runs the length of the rocket. Once the fuel is ignited, there is no stopping this kind of rocket. It burns at the maximum rate until all the fuel is spent. The burning fuel heats the air inside the channel, producing hot, pressurized gases that rush out the back of the rocket, propelling the rocket forward.

The propulsion of a liquid-fuel rocket engine is caused by hot, pressurized gases escaping from the engine, just as it is in the solid-fuel booster. But the liquid-fuel rocket contains fuel pumps and valves that control the rate of combustion. Like a conventional jet engine only much more powerful, a liquid-fuel rocket can speed up, slow down, or shut down altogether and start up again.

mankind, or more important for the long-range exploration of space."

It was the most daring dream of flight yet. Kennedy did not live to see the goal achieved. But 500,000,000 people, the largest television audience ever, watched the dream come true. On July 21, 1969, in an area of the moon called the Sea of Tranquility, U.S. astronaut Neil Armstrong became the first person to set foot on the moon. As he put it: "That's one small step for a man, one giant leap for mankind."

Following the successful moon flights, development of rocket-powered aircraft continued. By the early 1980s, the National Aeronautics and Space Administration (NASA) space shuttle *Challenger* was ready for its first flight. Designed with the wing structure of an airplane but powered by rockets, the *Challenger* in 1981 broke all the records for fixed-wing aircraft. Flying in the earth's orbit, *Challenger* reached the

Apollo 11 *commander Neil Armstrong sits in the Lunar module as it rests on the moon's surface.*

speed of 16,600 miles per hour at an altitude of 400,000 feet. Then *Challenger* set the record for time aloft when it stayed up for ten days and seven hours on its sixth mission in 1983.

Astronauts Neil Armstrong and Edwin Aldrin plant an American flag on the moon during the historic Apollo 11 *lunar landing on July 21, 1969.*

The rocket-powered Challenger *is prepared for take-off from Kennedy Space Center in Florida.*

But the *Challenger* flight the world remembers best was a disaster. On January 28, 1986, the shuttle exploded seventy-three seconds after lift-off, killing all seven crew members aboard. It was another grim reminder of the constant danger of flight.

Accepting that danger as a necessary risk, humans continue to explore the frontier of space. Scientists are making exciting plans as they prepare to further explore the reaches of our solar system and perhaps someday go beyond it. They dream of permanent colonies, where humans can live, work, and play in outer space. Such space stations would relieve some of the strain on the natural resources of the earth and help us discover greater resources

in space. For instance, some scientists predict that it will be possible to mine asteroids for minerals that are unavailable on earth.

Of course, the dream of such space exploits depend on further developing the flight technology we have now. The greatest hope for advancing this technology lies in inventing a new way to propel spacecraft. So far, all powered human aircraft, both for use in outer space and closer to the earth, have been fueled by the combustion of petroleum products or chemicals. With a limited supply of oil on earth, jet fuel will become more scarce and more expensive in the future. Rocket fuels are also tremendously expensive. At a cost of about one thousand dollars per pound,

TOMORROW'S LASER JET

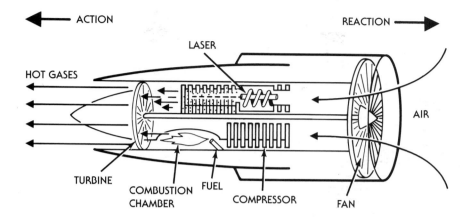

A laser jet engine would work like a conventional jet engine, but it would require only a small amount of liquid fuel for ignition. Once the engine was started, it would use a laser to heat the compressed air necessary to create propulsion.

the price of putting a one-hundred-ton aircraft into space soon becomes unaffordable.

The answer is to develop a cheap, readily available power source that would be useful on earth and in space. Some futurists predict that within a few decades, we will have aircraft powered by laser-driven engines. The laser (an acronym for light amplification by stimulated emission of radiation) is a device that creates and amplifies an intense beam of light. This concentrated beam of light consists of excited atoms that release photons, or particles of light. These photons, when emitted in a chain reaction, create a burst of radiation. Scientists think this energy can be used to power aircraft engines in the future. Laser-powered engines would be a revolutionary step forward in aircraft development.

In one scenario of future flight, scientists would power planes using laser beams from space. Mathematicians have found five special spots in the space between the earth and moon. Influenced by the gravitational pulls of these two celestial bodies, objects orbiting in these spots remain locked in the same position. Scientists could place huge power plants in these spots. They could be nuclear reactors, or they could collect and convert the abundant solar energy in outer space and then beam it in the form of a laser to aircraft below.

Some scientists predict that within a few decades, aircraft pilots will be able to request a power-generating laser beam that will follow the flight path of their aircraft. With a virtually inexhaustible supply of energy from the sun, these laser-powered aircraft would be inexpensive to use. A cheap form of transportation, they might eventually become available to everyone. Different models could be equipped for short hops around the neighborhood or for half-hour flights to almost any location on earth. On-board computers would coordinate with local traffic control to avoid collisions. Big passenger planes with several laser-receiving lenses located on top will probably look something like flying saucers. They will have several engines that use a mixture of hydrogen- and laser-powered rockets to propel them at hypersonic speeds—speeds greater than five times the speed of sound. These planes will reach up to Mach 15, at altitudes of up to 300,000 feet.

Compared to these dreams of future flying machines, the *Wright Flyer I* seems a quaint piece of clumsy machinery. Yet the first airplane was a revolutionary invention. As it evolved, it reshaped the boundaries of the world we live in.

The Wrights' creation was often used as a destructive force in the first half of the century. But humankind's capacity for flight has more recently become a cause for greater hope. Airplanes have played a part in helping people from different nations see that they do indeed share one world. The flying machine has made a major impact on world culture and cleared the way for huge changes still to come. We can see that Wilbur and Orville Wright took the first running steps for humankind's leap into space.

What will the future of human flight hold? The reply that Orville Wright once gave still holds true: "I cannot answer except to assure you that it will be spectacular."

Glossary

∎∎∎∎∎∎∎∎∎∎∎∎∎∎∎∎∎∎∎∎∎∎∎∎∎∎∎∎∎∎∎

aileron: A hinged or movable surface located on the trailing edge of an airplane wing.

alloy: A mixture of metals that often produces a stronger new metal.

altimeter: A device for measuring altitude above an agreed upon level, such as sea level. A radio altimeter measures the time it takes a radio wave to travel to earth and back to the airplane.

angle of attack: The angle at which the leading edge of an airplane's wings meets the wind.

barnstormer: Someone who independently flies a small plane, offering cheap rides and performing stunts, usually in rural areas.

compressor: A machine that reduces the volume of a gas, thus creating greater pressure.

elevator: A movable piece of the tail of an airplane; it controls the up and down movement of the plane.

equilibrium: A state of perfect balance.

fuselage: The body of the airplane, where passengers, cargo, engines, and equipment are held.

gyroscope: A device with a wheel that spins around an axis in such a way that the wheel maintains its own balance. Used to counteract rolling, it is part of an airplane's automatic steering system.

hydrodynamics: The study of the motion of fluids.

hydrogen: The simplest and lightest of the elements; a colorless, odorless, flammable gas.

kamikaze: A member of the Japanese air force of World War II assigned to commit suicide by crashing his plane into an enemy ship.

Luftwaffe: The German air force in World War II.

Mach number: The ratio of a body's speed to the speed of sound. Mach 2, for example, is twice the speed of sound.

meteorology: The study of the atmosphere, with regard to weather and its forecasting.

navigation: The science of guiding ships, aircraft, or spacecraft from place to place.

pitch: The up and down movement of a plane.

roll: The movement of a plane in which it turns over and over in a circular manner.

strut: A piece of wood, wire, or metal used in airplane construction; it strengthens and supports the airplane's wing.

supersonic: Speeds equal to the speed of sound (Mach 1) and up to five times

greater than the speed of sound
(Mach 5).

turbine: An rotary engine that spins as a result of a current of air.

turboprop: A jet engine that produces thrust by means of a turbine-driven propeller.

yaw: The side to side motion of a plane.

For Further Reading

Walter J. Boyne, *The Smithsonian Book of Flight.* New York: Orion, 1987.

Fred Howard, *Wilbur and Orville: A Biography of the Wright Brothers.* New York: Knopf, 1987.

Charles J. Kelly, Jr., *The Sky's the Limit: The History of the Airlines.* New York: Coward-McCann, 1963.

Leik Myrabo and Dean Ing, *The Future of Flight.* New York: Baen Publishing Enterprises, 1985.

Orville Wright, *How We Invented the Airplane.* New York: David McKay, 1953.

Melvin B. Zisfein, *Flight: A Panorama of Aviation.* New York: Pantheon, 1981.

Works Consulted

Richard Bach, *A Gift of Wings*. New York: Delacorte, 1974.

Roger E. Bilstein, *Flight in America, 1900–1983: From the Wrights to the Astronauts*. Baltimore, MD: Johns Hopkins University Press, 1984.

Roger E. Bilstein, *Flight Patterns: Trends of Aeronautical Development in the United States, 1918–1929*. Athens: University of Georgia Press, 1983.

John Blake, *Aviation, The First Seventy Years*. London: Tribune Books, 1973.

Joe Christy with Alexander T. Wells, *American Aviation: An Illustrated History*. Blue Ridge Summit, PA: TAB Books, 1987.

Donald C. Clarke, ed., *Aircraft and Airports*. New York: Arco, 1978.

Harry Combs with Martin Caidin, *Kill Devil Hill: Discovering the Secret of the Wright Brothers*. Boston: Houghton Mifflin, 1979.

Joseph J. Corn, *The Winged Gospel: America's Romance with Aviation, 1900–1950*. New York: Oxford University Press, 1983.

Heiner Emde, *Conquerors of the Air: The Evolution of Aircraft 1903–1945*. New York: Viking, 1968.

H. Guyford Stever et al., *Flight*. New York: Time-Life Inc., 1965.

Index

About the Author

The author, Tom Stacey, is a graduate of
Michigan State University. He has worked as a
reporter and editor for several West Coast
newspapers, and now lives and works as a
freelance writer in La Jolla, California.

Picture Credits

■ ■

Cover photo by Eric Meola/The Image
  Bank
AP/Wide World Photos, 61 (both), 63
  (bottom), 64 (top left & right), 65, 69
  (top), 74 (middle & bottom), 77 (both),
  78, 79, 81
British Airways, 75 (bottom)
Lear Jet Corporation, 75 (top)
National Aeronautics and Space
  Administration, 72 (right), 83 (both),
  84 (both)
Smithsonian Institution, 12, 13, 14, 15
  (both), 17, 19 (all), 20 (all), 21 (both),
  22, 23, 25 (both), 26, 27, 29 (both), 31,
  33, 34 (both), 35 (all), 36, 38, 39, 40, 41,
  42, 44 (both), 46, 47, 48, 50 (all), 51, 52,
  53, 54, 55, 57 (both), 60, 62, 63 (top), 64
  (bottom), 68 (both), 69 (bottom), 71
  (both), 72 (left), 74 (top)
U.S. Air Force photo, 70, 73
Lawrence E. Wilson, 59